PRAISE FOR

Sensitive
Is the
NEW STRONG

"Moorjani teaches you to embrace your sensitivity and see it as a strength, and she shows you how to empower yourself and become the leader of your life, while showing us all how sensitivity is a valuable and needed component in our future evolution. I highly recommend this book for all empaths and their loved ones."

—JACK CANFIELD, #1 *New York Times* bestselling coauthor of the Chicken Soup for the Soul series

"*Sensitive Is the New Strong* is the absolute truth of what it's like to live as an empath. It teaches us how to understand that our inherent sensitivity is not a liability; it's a strength. If you've ever been told to toughen up or just get over it, this book is for you. I believe that empaths are the new normal. And it's time that we finally learned how to step into the superpower that has always existed within."

—CHRISTIANE NORTHRUP, MD, *New York Times* bestselling author of *Women's Bodies, Women's Wisdom*

"Thank you so much, Anita Moorjani, for writing this book and for shining the way for all of us, especially empaths, to recapture our dormant—and most important—sixth sense. There is so much possible and never a better time."

—PAM GROUT, #1 *New York Times* bestselling author of *E-Squared* and *The Course in Miracles Experiment*

"Fabulous insights on how to live from the heart of an empath like no other. Anita's views on six-sensory living, and thriving, with an emphasis on self-appreciation, are out of this world. This treasure is a love story, about you."

—MIKE DOOLEY, *New York Times*
bestselling author of *Infinite Possibilities*

"Anita Moorjani has done it again! *Sensitive Is the New Strong* is a gorgeous and powerful field guide to the empath living in today's wild world. If you, like millions of others, struggle with emotional regulation, overwhelm, and holding healthy boundaries, get ready to feel truly seen . . . and to learn how to express gifts you may not even realize you have from a place of power and grace."

—LAURA BERMAN, PhD,
author of *Quantum Love*

"Whether you're an artist or an engineer, a homemaker or policy maker, *Sensitive Is the New Strong* will catapult you beyond the casual speculation of what intuition and empathy can mean in your life to reveal the practical steps that you can take now to unveil the most intimate relationship that you'll ever experience—your relationship with yourself and your personal power."

—GREGG BRADEN, *New York Times*
bestselling author of *Human by Design*
and *The God Code*

"*Sensitive Is the New Strong* is a book that provides YOU with groundbreaking information, tools, and exercises in understanding the challenges faced by empaths. You can learn how to protect your energy and thrive. A definite must-read for empaths and their loved ones."

—NICK ORTNER, *New York Times*
bestselling author of *The Tapping Solution*

"*Sensitive Is the New Strong* is a practical user's manual for the gifted empath who must learn to balance their inner world of thoughts and feelings with their outer material world. Anita Moorjani gives us the knowledge and the tools to free ourselves to live a more meaningful life. This book is for anyone who is courageous enough to feel."

—DR. JOE DISPENZA, *New York Times*
bestselling author of *You Are the Placebo*

"For every last people pleaser who feels too much and takes too little, this is the essential handbook."

—LYNNE McTAGGART, internationally
bestselling author of *The Intention Experiment*

"The key to planetary sustainability—indeed, the survival of the human race—does not lie in our becoming more ruthless. It lies in our ability for kindness, empathy, wisdom, and collaboration. Moorjani gives the why and the how of the new meaning of strong."

—MARIANNE WILLAMSON, *New York Times*
bestselling author of *A Return to Love*

"Many empaths have no idea that they are empaths—this insightful and practical book will help them identify themselves, and reveal their importance to the world."

—EBEN ALEXANDER, MD, author of
Living in a Mindful Universe

"This is a remarkable, insightful book that will speak to empaths all over the world. I thought I was reading about myself as I turned each new page. I truly loved reading this book and will be recommending it to all my empath friends."

—DAVID R. HAMILTON, PHD, bestselling author
of *How Your Mind Can Heal Your Body*

"Moorjani's revealing insights will appeal to her many fans as well as those just beginning to understand their empathic abilities."

—*Publishers Weekly*

"The essential guidebook for those of us who are tired of seeing our sensitivity as a detriment and who instead want to harness its power and strength."

—*Ms.* magazine

ALSO BY ANITA MOORJANI

BOOKS

What If This Is Heaven? How Our Cultural Myths
Prevent Us from Experiencing Heaven on Earth

Dying to Be Me: My Journey from Cancer, to Near Death, to True Healing

Hmm... What Do You Know About Who You Really Are

CDS AND MP3S

The New Earth Experience: Conscious Meditation

Listening to Departmental Journey

Sensitive
Is the
NEW STRONG

The Power of Empaths

in an Increasingly Harsh World

ANITA MOORJANI

ENLIVEN BOOKS

ATRIA

NEW YORK   LONDON   TORONTO   SYDNEY   NEW DELHI

ENLIVEN
ATRIA

An Imprint of Simon & Schuster, Inc.
1230 Avenue of the Americas
New York, NY 10020

First Enliven Books/Atria Paperback edition March 2022

ENLIVEN BOOKS **/ATRIA** PAPERBACK and colophon are trademarks of Simon & Schuster, Inc.

For information about special discounts for bulk purchases, please contact Simon & Schuster Special Sales at 1-866-506-1949 or business@simonandschuster.com.

The Simon & Schuster Speakers Bureau can bring authors to your live event. For more information or to book an event, contact the Simon & Schuster Speakers Bureau at 1-866-248-3049 or visit our website at www.simonspeakers.com.

Interior design by Kyoko Watanabe

3 5 7 9 10 8 6 4 2

Library of Congress Cataloging-in-Publication Data

Names: Moorjani, Anita, 1959- author.
Title: Sensitive is the new strong : the power of empaths in an increasingly harsh world / Anita Moorjani.
Description: First hardcover edition. | New York, NY : Atria Books, [2021] | Summary: "The New York Times bestselling author of Dying to Be Me returns with an inspirational guide for sensitive people looking to fully harness their gifts of intuition and empathy in today's harsh world"—Provided by publisher.
Identifiers: LCCN 2020044384 (print) | LCCN 2020044385 (ebook) | ISBN 9781501196676 (hardcover) | ISBN 9781501196683 (paperback) | ISBN 9781501196690 (ebook)
Subjects: LCSH: Sensitivity (Personality trait) | Empathy. | Resilience (Personality trait)
Classification: LCC BF698.35.S47 M66 2021 (print) | LCC BF698.35.S47 (ebook) | DDC 155.2/32—dc23
LC record available at https://lccn.loc.gov/2020044384
LC ebook record available at https://lccn.loc.gov/2020044385

ISBN 978-1-5011-9667-6
ISBN 978-1-5011-9668-3 (pbk)
ISBN 978-1-5011-9669-0 (ebook)

DEDICATION

To the gentler souls who walk among us; the sensitive, empathetic ones who give of themselves tirelessly without a thought for their own needs; the self-sacrificing among us who don't know how to receive.

These gentle souls include those who say "yes" even when they feel like saying "no"; who are in service to everyone except themselves; who feel guilty when they take care of themselves; who have been victimized and bullied; who have no idea of their own self-worth.

You have silenced your voice and made yourself small so others can feel big, and have dimmed your light for so long that you don't know how to shine anymore.

You've read all the spiritual books, all the self-help books. You've prayed, meditated, chanted, forgiven everyone who's wronged you and forgiven them again, only to find that while you've been so engaged, the world outside has been hijacked by the louder and more aggressive voices among us.

This book is for you. Your voice is vital and your light is essential. It's time to step into your truth and take back your soul, your life, and your world.

CONTENTS

CONTENTS

PART III:
Your Relationship with the World

Sensitive
Is the
NEW STRONG

INTRODUCTION

Have you ever seen a child fall down and skin her knee—and felt it in your own body? Have you ever been with a friend who's feeling anxious or distressed, and felt the same discomfort? Do you feel drained around certain people? Anxious in a crowd? Sense when someone's not telling you the truth? Have you ever said "Yes" to a request when every cell in your body was shouting "NO!"? Have you been told you're "too sensitive," "too emotional," "weak," or that you "care too much?" Have you been asked, "Why can't you be like everyone else?"

If your answer to these questions is yes, then like me and so many of the people I talk to every day, the likelihood is that you're an empath, a highly sensitive person who feels and absorbs the thoughts, emotions, and energy of others.

Empaths have a unique way of viewing and sensing the world—we feel things more deeply. We have a highly developed intuition. We assume that everyone sees the world as we do, but in fact, most don't, and because of that, we feel odd, different. The lines between ourselves and others are often blurred, and we're chastised, bullied, and made to feel flawed or ashamed. We're told to "grow a thicker skin" and "be stronger," and if you're a guy, you've likely heard: "Man up" and "Boys/Men don't cry."

Criticism and disapproval hurt us more than most. To avoid the pain and to fit in, we often mold ourselves into what we believe others want us to be. As a result, we can become people-pleasers and what I affectionately refer to as doormats (both are just phases, not who you are). And because of the fear of ridicule, being bullied, or not fitting in, we also hide our gifts, and in doing so, our true selves, until we don't know who we are anymore.

I believe that every decision we make, every choice, either takes us a step forward, toward expressing and accepting our most authentic selves, or takes us a step back, toward losing ourselves, toward being small, and ultimately toward dis-ease. I grew up in a culture where I was rewarded for being nonconfrontational, invisible, and a people-pleaser. I made myself small to the point of invisibility and always felt the need to apologize even for my own existence. So many empaths I speak with feel this way. When our history, our roots, are embedded in a world where we've been rewarded for being nonconfrontational people-pleasers, it can become incredibly frustrating to feel unable to speak out, both on our own behalf and about the many injustices around us.

Much healing is needed on our planet. Ours is a world in peril. If you watch or read the news each day, or are active on social media, you wouldn't be faulted for fearing that we may possibly be on the verge of our own extinction. Just look at everything the media reports on—all the shootings, killings, the political wars, and the way people rip one another apart and speak about one another. People are getting angrier. We're stressed. We can't have a conversation without it becoming political. As I write this, we're dealing with the COVID-19 pandemic. And while the Internet has brought so much good to our lives, it's also amplified all that's going on around us. It seems that every single incident, everywhere on the planet, is reported in real time, 24/7. There are no rules, no codes of conduct, and this world can feel oppressive and overwhelming.

For empaths, today's world is a minefield. We often want to scream at those in power—those who uphold the idea of "survival of the fittest" and use whatever means to get to the top—to stop spreading fear and instead spread compassion, but that very act of speaking out runs counter to what we've been conditioned to do and be. Speaking out publicly not only requires tremendous courage, but it also opens us up to blatant attacks, which we may feel ill-equipped to handle. So the thought of adding our voices to the conversation is enough to make us run and hide under a rock.

Yet there's also never been a better time for empaths to emerge.

Empaths uphold the traits we as a culture have gradually lost in past years: sensitivity, empathy, kindness, and compassion. Empaths have always existed and, with the present state of our world, more books are being written to help us; as a result, not only are more people becoming aware that they *are* empaths, but the number very well may be growing.

Christiane Northrup, MD, author of *Dodging Energy Vampires* and an empath herself, writes, "Empaths are highly advanced souls being incarnated on earth in increasing numbers to shed light into the darkness during this time of transformation."[1]

That's why I've titled this book *Sensitive Is the New Strong*.

When I realized I was an empath, I had no toolbox to dig into, no appliances to assist me or instruction manuals to read—nothing to help me transition from *invisible* to *obvious*. I soon realized that if there were going to be a toolbox to take the person I used to be to who I am now, I would have to create that toolbox for myself. And that's what I did.

The tools and suggestions I offer in this book are not the type of tips you may have read before. I'm not going to tell you how to build rock-solid boundaries and shield yourself from others. This book isn't about walls, barriers, and protection. If we hide behind walls to protect ourselves, we'll never go out into the world and shine our light.

This book is about expansion, liberation, and connection with your own divinity. It's about speaking out, honoring yourself, and loving yourself. It's about embracing all that you are, chipping away at what you're not; about undoing, not doing. Once you learn how to honor and develop your own gifts, I encourage you to get out there, shine your empathic light, take on leadership roles, and become role models!

I've divided this book into three parts: The World of an Empath, Your Relationship with Yourself, and Your Relationship with the World. Each chapter includes my journey from wrestling with a specific challenge to eventually embracing the sensitivity that defines me today, as well as anecdotes and stories from my students, my readers, and my friends and family, all of whom have had their own journeys to tread. Out of this came a path that I hope will inspire and inform you to forge your own way out of feeling small, and help you to see how you can be leaders, healers, and agents of change in your own way.

In these pages, in addition to the stories, I offer information, exercises, and tools that have helped me embrace my gifts and honor who I am. You'll learn what it means to be an empath, and we'll explore the hurdles empaths face, as well as the gifts, or superpowers, we possess. In doing so, you'll understand that there's nothing wrong with you. You'll realize your strengths, and find guidance to help you rise from a place of victimhood and doormat-hood into a place of power. You'll learn to accept and nurture your unique sensitivity rather than letting it stunt or harm you.

Reading these pages, you'll learn how to turn inward for guidance, rather than outward. You'll discover how doormats are made and how to stop doormat-hood in its tracks; how to stop saying "yes" when every fiber of your being is screaming "no"; and how to protect yourself from illness and take part in your own healing. We'll also explore money—how to embrace earning what you're worth as a way of stepping into your power, valuing yourself and your work, and helping others on the planet.

At the beginning of each chapter, I've included a mantra, as a way of encapsulating and integrating the focus, while at the end of each chapter, I've created a short meditation to help you integrate the lessons of that chapter in that deeper space of your subconscious. I invite you to carve out twenty minutes of time and find a quiet space. Take four deep breaths before repeating the words slowly and silently in your mind or out loud for eight repetitions, with four breaths in between each. Once done, close your eyes for about five to seven minutes, allowing the words to sink in.

You may wish to journal any insights that come to you during the process. Don't fret if nothing comes to you the first few times you do the meditations. It's likely many of you have blocked your intuition for years, so you may need to exercise that muscle again.

If you know you're an empath but don't quite know how to marshal your gifts as strengths; suspect you're an empath and want to learn more; are drawn to this topic but haven't self-identified as an empath; or believe one of your loved ones is an empath, this book is for you.

I invite you to imagine experiencing yourself and the world in a whole new way, from a place of love rather than one of fear, expansion rather than retraction, connectedness rather than isolation. What would it be like to show up more authentically, empowered and fully connected to your intuition and your deepest purpose?

Are you ready?

Then let's dive right in!

PART I

The World of an Empath

Chapter 1

ARE YOU AN EMPATH?

MANTRA:
"I am a soul, not a role."

L ying on my mat, breathing in a mist of frankincense and neroli oils, I slowly opened my eyes, just enough to peek at the ceremony going on around me. The shaman circled the forty other participants in the cabin, chanting mantras in his native tongue that echoed and reverberated off the high-vaulted ceilings. For several minutes he waved a burning sage stick over each person in a circular motion while an assistant sprayed the air with liquid that smelled like the plant-based aromatherapy oils I burned at home. Another assistant waved a wand that looked like a deer horn, drawing patterns in the thick smoke created by the burning sage. This ritual was designed, we were told, to clear us of any unwanted energies that we were inadvertently carrying around in our bodies—energies accumulated from urban living that could eventually lead to exhaustion, stress, and depression.

I closed my eyes and, within minutes, I heard the shaman, followed by his dancing, drumming, incense-waving assistants, approach me. I sensed him looking down at me. Then, with the smell of burning sage overwhelmingly thick and strong, a deep voice whispered in my ear, "Get up and come with me."

Dressed in white and wreathed in white feathers, his two assistants by his side, he beckoned me to get up and follow him. I looked around the room. Everyone was still lying on their mats in a trance.

As the two assistants held the drumbeat steady and chanted to sustain the altered state of the others, I followed the shaman to the front of the room, which was dark, aside from a few flickering candles. I'd known this would be an all-night affair, but I'd lost track of time. Was it two o'clock in the morning? Three? And why, here in this huge cabin in the middle of the Costa Rican jungle (where I'd planned to relax but instead found myself, at the urging of two friends and spurred on by my own curiosity) at a type of ceremony I'd never attended, had I been singled out?

The shaman sat in a large wicker chair, the back of which towered over him and fanned out like a peacock's tail. He signaled for me to sit on the floor in front of him. As I took a seat, I felt both apprehensive and excited. *What would he say?*

"It looks to me like you need a special healing," he said. "I'd like to perform that for you."

Why me?

"You are different," he said, as if reading my mind. "You have a special purpose here, and I can sense that you need some help."

He asked me to close my eyes, then put his hands on my head and started chanting again. He then asked me to lie down on the ground as he sprinkled the frankincense/neroli–scented liquid over me in a ritual that proceeded for another twenty minutes. Finally, he told me to sit up. I felt light-headed and unsettled.

"You have a special purpose," he eventually said again, "but you haven't been developing it to the best of your ability. You have been absorbing a lot of energy that is not yours. Tell me, has something unusual happened to you in your life? You are different. Your energy is different from others. You have a gift, but you have buried it."

In fact, something quite unusual *had* happened in my life. I told the shaman how I'd almost died from cancer several years earlier. I told him about the near-death experience (NDE) that had saved my life. I explained how, after I came back from my NDE, I went on to talk and write about it. The late, great Dr. Wayne Dyer had discovered my life story and encouraged me to write my first book, *Dying to Be Me,* which put me on the world stage in 2011. Deep down, I had this inner knowing that this was my calling—my destiny—to share what I'd learned with the world. Wrapped within the message of self-love I felt compelled to deliver was the importance of being fearlessly authentic, speaking our truth, and being, unapologetically, who we are. We are, after all, expressions of divinity.

But after the publication of my first book, I was suddenly thrust into the international spotlight on a massive scale, into a life that was bigger than I'd ever imagined; and although it felt so *right*—it felt like the life I was meant to live—it was also a life I'd never been socialized to deal with.

You see, in the past, before my NDE, I was invisible. I contorted myself emotionally to please other people, denied my own needs, said "yes" when I wanted to say "no," and dimmed my own light to gain people's approval or avoid disappointing them. I was also supersensitive—so sensitive that I often experienced other people's emotional or physical pain in my own body. In fact, I was sometimes even *more* sensitive to other people's feelings than I was to my own, putting myself last even to the point of apologizing for my own existence!

There was nowhere to hide and no reason to hide, but the experience was more complex than I could possibly have imagined. Tens of thousands of people wanted information from me about healing; they wanted wisdom, solace, and connection. I deeply wanted to help every single person who reached out to me, but it wasn't possible because there was only one of me. And that fact alone—that I might let anyone down or disappoint anyone in any way—pained me even more.

"You got a second chance at life and the gift of being healed," the shaman said in the cabin, looking me squarely in the face. "Your near-death experience tuned you into the energies around you, which is what healed you. This is a big gift—but it is also a challenge and a responsibility, because you are very sensitive to both the powerful healing energies as well as those that are detrimental to your well-being. It is not your job to absorb everyone else's energy. It is not your job to rescue people at your expense or convince them of what is possible if they don't believe you. Your only job is to empower yourself, to stay connected to your center, and allow your presence to inspire others so they know what is possible in order to heal, if it's their fate to do so."

I sat there, hanging on every word the shaman said. No one had addressed me in this way before, with such clarity and conviction, about my state of being.

"If you do not consciously stay centered," the shaman said, "you will end up absorbing other people's energies whenever you help them. I have just cleared your energy in this ceremony. If I hadn't done that, you could have gotten another serious illness like you did the first time." My eyes widened at the thought. "You need to protect yourself," he continued. "You have a greater purpose to complete here. Greater than you are currently aware of. Your second chance was a gift—a gift of understanding and an opportunity. Don't waste this gift."

The power of his words resonated with me on every level and underscored an urgent life question: If this gift of mine is a blessing and a curse, a sort of double-edged sword, how can I empower myself and stay centered? How do I take the knowledge that came to me during my NDE and truly live it? How do I protect myself yet keep an open heart to better serve others as well as myself? How does *anyone* with the same keen and sometimes overwhelming sensitivity to life *own* their power? Personally, I didn't know how to be any other way. I had no tools. But clearly, the shaman saw something.

Here's what took place during my NDE.

February 2, 2006 was supposed to have been the last day of my life. That was the day doctors told my family that I was in the final stages of Hodgkin's lymphoma, a form of lymphatic cancer. The cancer ravaging my body had metastasized and spread from the base of my skull to my breasts, under my arms, and all the way to my abdomen. My lungs were filled with fluid and I was no longer absorbing nutrition. I was in a coma as my organs began shutting down. Death was upon me.

But suddenly, while in the process of dying—completely aware of the urgency of the medical team, the frenzied emotions of my family, the doctor's words ("Her heart may be beating but it's too late to save her")—I experienced something so infinite and altogether fantastic that I titled an entire chapter in *Dying to Be Me* with those very words: "Something Infinite and Altogether Fantastic." There's no other way to describe it. In short, even though my physical body had died, I, my soul, my essence, my Being, wasn't dead! I felt amazing—light, and free. The pain and fear were gone. The fear from the illness that had been ravaging my body, and the fear of death—all gone.

I was aware of the vastness, complexity, and depth of everything around me, while being simultaneously aware that I was part of something alive, infinite, and altogether fantastic—a large and unfolding tapestry beyond sight and sound. It was a place of total clarity, where everything made sense. I could intrinsically see and feel how we're all connected and part of the same consciousness. I could also understand how every thought and every decision I had made in my life up to that point had led me to that moment, lying on that hospital bed, dying of cancer.

Eventually, I reached a point in this transcendent state where I had to make a choice: Do I come back to this physical body or do I continue on to this other realm? At first, not one single fiber in my being wanted to come back. Why would I want to leave this amazing space? Suddenly, however, I sensed the presence of my dad, who had died ten years prior. He was there to help me through this transition. "It's not your time," he said. "You have some gifts waiting for you, so you need to go back to your physical body."

"But why would I want to go back to a sick and dying body?" I protested.

We didn't communicate verbally, of course, because we have no biology in the other realm. Still, there was no boundary between my father's pure essence and mine, despite us not having been particularly close when I was growing up in the physical realm. I just *knew* what he wanted me to know. Even the term "telepathic communication" isn't strong enough to describe that communication. My dad wanted me to know that now that I'd experienced the truth of who I really was and had clarity about what had caused the cancer, the cancer would heal if I chose to go back to my body. The moment I made the decision to return to this physical plane was the moment my dad said to me, "Go back and live your life fearlessly."

I returned to my physical body, opened my eyes, and came out of the coma. Within five weeks the doctors could find no trace of cancer in my body. Except to acknowledge that it was nothing short of a miracle, they couldn't explain what had happened.

Empaths Are Different

When I returned home from my trip to Costa Rica, I researched information about how to protect myself and set boundaries, and one word kept coming up over and over again: "empath." I was familiar with the word but had never paid much attention to it. Even when a few people had suggested to me in the past that I was, in fact, an empath, I'd dismissed it as a label, because right or wrong, I'm not fond of labels. But at that point I was curious, so I researched it in the most mundane possible way—I took an online quiz! Lo and behold, I scored twenty-nine out of thirty. An online quiz may not seem very scientific, but if you source it from someone reliable, it can give you the language you need to start to access your own vulnerabilities and strengths. In this book, I will take you much deeper than any commercial quiz can go, but you can use something this simple and accessible as a starting place. Also, you can take my quiz at the end of this chapter (and on my website).

The results of the quiz drove me to do more research. I read books and articles about empaths, and as I read through the articles I truly started to understand, for the first time, why I struggle with standing firm in who I am. I came to understand that being an empath wasn't a condition I could get rid of, so I needed to stop judging myself and beating myself up for being this way. Instead, I had to learn to accept it, love it, and work with it. I also understood why I struggled with coping in the world. It was because I was living in a world where the majority of the people didn't experience it in the same way I did.

This understanding opened up a whole new way of looking at myself and others, and that's when I started to realize that many of those who are attracted to my work are empaths themselves. I started asking for a show of hands at my events to determine how many people identified themselves as empaths, and about 80 to 90 percent of my audience usually raised their hands. There were many who hadn't heard the term or didn't know what it meant, so I would read out a list of traits, and then ask again, and more hands would go up. I was amazed by this. I made a commitment to myself to learn more about navigating life as an empath and developing tools, not just for myself, but to help all the other empaths out there.

Before I dive into the world and traits of empaths, let me first say that you don't have to die, as I did, to awaken these abilities. You can access these gifts at any time in your life. Some of us have been empaths our whole life and didn't know it, or didn't have a name for it. Others might not be full-on empaths but have many traits that fall into the spectrum of sensitivities that make us very different from other people.

Very different from other people. It's hard for me to even write these words, since one of the profound takeaways from my NDE was that, on a transcendent level, we are all made of the same substance. When we shed our physical bodies, we are all pure essence, pure love, pure divinity, and pure spirituality. We are all interconnected. Yet in our physical bodies, it's by embracing our differences that we truly feel that connection with us all the time. When we embrace our differences—and others and their differences—we're honoring the multifaceted consciousness of the all that is.

I believe that this interconnectedness is our fundamental nature, but we forget this truth when we inhabit our physical bodies on this earthly plane. Each one of us who is born into this physical world will experience a specific set of circumstances. And these circumstances—our families, our culture, our upbringing, and countless lived experiences—inform our personalities and our psychology (a concept that I'll explore in greater detail in pages to come). I believe that at our core, we are all fundamentally *good*, doing our best with what we know. I don't think we deliberately set out to hurt others or cause harm. We only cause harm out of ignorance, fear, or when we're in survival mode, and from that place, we believe (rightly or wrongly) that there's no other option to deal with the circumstances we're facing, and in imposing our will or beliefs, we restrict other people's way of dealing with the circumstances.

Be that as it may, through these life circumstances, we accumulate layers of fears, anger, and social conditioning that bring on a sort of amnesia, both individual and collective, about who we truly are. And for the empath, this amnesia can be hugely detrimental. Our unusual sensitivity can easily become the double-edged sword the shaman had referred to: both a blessing and a curse.

It's important to understand the difference between being sensitive and being an empath. Dr. Elaine Aron was one of the first people to describe the world of the highly sensitive person, which later became known by its acronym "HSP," as used in her ground-breaking book *The Highly Sensitive Person*. According to Dr. Aron, 15 to 20 percent of the population are HSPs, with nervous systems that are biologically different.[1] Of those HSPs, a smaller percentage are also empaths. Empaths share all the traits of HSPs but have a much more intense experience. Dr. Judith Orloff later explored the world of the empath in her book *The Empath's Survival Guide*, where she explained that empaths not only feel but absorb the positive and negative energies around us. "We don't have the same filters that other people do to block out stimulation. . . . We are so sensitive," she explains, "that it's like holding something in a hand that has fifty fingers instead of five."[2]

I see the difference between HSPs and empaths in my own life. My husband, Danny, is super intuitive, and can easily sense people's needs even before they've voiced them. He's a natural caretaker. However, he's not an empath because he doesn't seem to absorb their energies into his own field. He doesn't need everyone around him to feel good in order to feel good himself, whereas I need people around me to feel good or they affect my well-being. This is another reason why empaths are prone to becoming people-pleasers—they need the people around them to feel good in order to feel good themselves, so they're constantly rescuing and helping people.

I'm always getting comments on my social media platforms and from my audience at events saying that their emotions are constantly on overload because they're continually helping or rescuing others, and struggle with saying no. They also struggle with taking care of their own needs, because it always seems that others' needs are more urgent or important than their own.

In fact, empaths can even experience the energetic fields around other people. It's almost as if we're able to tune in to multiple radio stations at the same time, though it can be difficult to differentiate between *our* station—what's being broadcast to us from our own North Star, if you will—and the stations of others. This creates static, confusion, and even exhaustion, as the needs of other people eclipse our own and we absorb their frequency and energy.

Add to this the fact that people with problems—those who need a shoulder to cry on—often flock toward empaths because we are a rare breed: We're highly sensitive creatures who *truly listen* to them and understand their pain. We empaths are rescuers, givers, and healers. It deeply hurts us to see others suffer. We literally *feel* what they feel. The downside of this gift is that when we're unaware of the depth of our sensitivities, we give our power away and exhaust our emotional and physical resources—the end result being that we can be the best healers for others, but the worst for ourselves.

The insights I had during my near-death experience made it clear to me that I'm in a unique position to develop a guide for those of us who are empaths. I fully believe that not understanding how to live as an empath (and not even knowing I *was* an empath!), or how I was taking on the energy of others at the expense of myself (and hiding who I really was), nearly killed me. I experienced firsthand what can happen when we let go of all our self-judgment and doubt, our need for love and approval from outside ourselves. I also learned that the secret is to embrace all that we are, to live our lives fully, fearlessly, and out loud—which is often tough for empaths. And I experienced the amazing lives we can have when we do. I realized that I'm an expression of the divine, that we all are. I just never knew it before, so I'd never allowed myself to express myself fully, always thinking, "Who am I to speak up/go for what I want/ break convention?" Or I'd second-guess myself. I put other people first and believed that everybody else was more important, more qualified. The NDE made me realize that as an expression of the divine, I was here for a purpose, and to deny expressing myself meant denying a facet of the divine from expressing *itself* in this reality.

Imagine the lives we can have when we realize we are truly aspects of the divine. Imagine living your life from the place of knowing that you are a facet of the all that is. Imagine living from that place of knowing. We all can.

Living as a Six-Sensory Being
in a Five-Sensory World

I believe that we're born as six-sensory beings—that is, having an intuitive awareness inexplicable in terms of normal five-sensory perception. This awareness can include traits such as clairvoyance (perceiving objects not apparent to the five senses) and precognition (foreseeing future events), and being an empath, among others. Due to life circumstances, many people lose their innate connection to that sixth sense. We've all had the experience of knowing something before it happens or knowing when something more is going on in a situation than meets the eye. That's called intuition—knowing what's true. This is the bedrock of the empath's abilities. But many of us lose touch with this gift of intuition. Those who share any such sixth-sensory traits seem to come into this world with a deep inner knowing of our connection to one another and to the Universe (more in Chapter 3), but we're discouraged from trusting our intuition as we grow up, and ultimately we often disregard it or suppress it.

For this reason, many empaths don't even know they possess this sixth sense. I certainly didn't—but the NDE blew my sixth sense right open again, and I realized that it was real, and was something I'd always had. And though I'd completely forgotten about this aspect of myself, when it came back, it felt so familiar. I even started to wonder how I'd managed to live my life without it all those years.

You, too, may have had an experience that blasted open your sixth sense. It can occur because of a necessity (someone needs help, or you need help yourself), or a trauma, but sometimes people just wake up and realize it's back, or they begin to feel it for the first time.

We're born with a strong intuitive connection to everything and everyone around us, but we live in a world that barely acknowledges our sixth sense. However, for some of us, our inner knowing is as strong, or maybe even stronger, than our other senses—like our sense of hearing or sight. Think about babies, and how they immediately sense the presence of their mother, even before their eyes are open; or pets, and how they sense the arrival of their keeper well before he or she is within earshot or line of sight.

I had a dog, Cosmo, who used to station himself at my front door exactly five minutes before I walked in, every single time. Whatever he was doing, and wherever he was in the house, when I was five minutes away, he'd leave his spot and perch by the door. Whoever was home would know I'd walk through that door in five minutes. When I say five minutes away, I mean five minutes by car, which is about a mile away, so there was no way he could have smelled, seen, or heard me. We lived in an apartment building, and when I would step into the elevator on the ground floor, Cosmo would start wagging his tail from his spot behind the closed door of our apartment. Danny and I used to have so much fun marveling at Cosmo's incredibly sharp intuition.

As a culture, we've been conditioned to believe that our intuition isn't real, that it's part of our imagination, if you will. Maybe as a child you had imaginary friends who actually were very real to you, but your family laughed and told you they were just a figment of your imagination. Or maybe your parents were trying to get you to hug a particular relative or friend, and when you sensed their intentions were less than good and shied away, your parents pushed you toward them, telling you not to be so shy or rude. How did that make you feel about yourself? That certainly happened to me, and I often felt ashamed, different, confused. In the end, I would bury the incident *and* my intuition—an experience with which I'm sure many of you can identify. I often receive mail from people sharing their own stories about how they've had to suppress that part of themselves, because when they expressed it, they were told it was just their imagination; they were laughed at or bullied by their peers for being different; or they were punished at home or at school—and how painful that suppression was.

Our sixth sense is as real as the other five. Let's explore this idea for a moment. If you were without one of those five senses, you would definitely notice its absence. Just imagine if, from the time you were born, you were told to keep your eyes closed. You were told that it's dangerous to open your eyes and see the world around you. Although you would have developed great intuition to compensate for your lack of sight—an inner vision—you would not have the gift of seeing the beauty of this world as perceived by the human eye.

This would mean you'd never seen colors, or the sky, or a rainbow. You would never have seen rivers or mountains or trees or stars or clouds. Let's say that as a child, every now and again, you forgot to keep your eyes closed, so you glimpsed what the world looked like, and you told the adults around you about what you saw. But they dismissed you and said, "It's your imagination. You've got to keep your eyes closed if you want to navigate this world!" Imagine how different that world would be. All our inventions, all of our technology, would be geared toward helping us navigate the world with our eyes closed.

So you learned to keep your eyes closed because you wanted to fit in. You didn't want to disappoint people. You grew up as a five-sensory being, except those senses—intuition, hearing, smell, touch, and taste—did not include sight. You went through school, where everybody, even the teachers, had their eyes closed. You graduated, got a job, and began your career as someone with their eyes closed. You lived in a world created by people without sight, for people without sight; so intuition was strong, but people couldn't see. Or they *could* see, if they believed in sight, if they opened their eyes.

Now imagine one day, as an adult, you remember that as a child you could see things! You remember there was another sense you had, but you were told it was your imagination. You vaguely remember what the world outside looked like, and you want to find that sense again. You long for that glimpse of something greater. So you decide to experiment and tune back into the world that you explored as a child.

You're outside, playing. The grass is greener than you remember. You can see the babbling brook, instead of just hearing it. You can see the rocks and shrubs in your path and easily avoid hurting yourself. You can see into the distance and measure how far away a mountain is just by sight! Where you've always been able to tell how far away the ocean is by smell, now you can actually see it, too. You can see how the color of water changes, the farther away from the shore it is, and how, where it's closer, where sand meets sea, its translucent—a concept you've never been able to understand before.

Think of the clarity. Think of how differently you'd navigate the world with this new sense.

So now that you've made this discovery, imagine that you go around telling people, "Open your eyes. It's amazing! There's a whole sixth sense that we have, which we've suppressed since we were children. But it's real! You can access it, too! There's nothing to be afraid of. It will actually make your life better and easier."

You're so excited about the discovery that you want to shout it from the rooftops. "Actually, guys, you can open your eyes. Life will be easier." But people are saying to you, "No. You can't open your eyes. It's disrespectful and goes against everything that we've been brought up to believe." They tell you that you're a threat to all the technology that's being developed, that's generating revenue and jobs. People insist that you close your eyes again. And you're wondering, *How can so many people be wrong? So many people in authority are telling me that I am. I must have imagined it. I don't want to take a risk!* You don't want to take the risk of being ostracized for being different.

There's also the fear of the unknown. Because no one else has their eyes open, there's no information available to you about the possible risks or pitfalls, if any, of navigating life with your eyes open. And if you're the only one perceiving the world in this way, you'll start to feel lonely. There will be no words. Language is developed by a mutual agreement of what meaning to assign to vocal sounds, but if everyone has their eyes closed, there will be no words assigned to properties that can only be identified visually. For example, there will be no way to assign a name to each color in the spectrum if no one can see them.

You will eventually begin to realize that you live in a world created *by* people with their eyes closed, *for* people with their eyes closed. No one will understand you, because you're perceiving something no one else has perceived, with no words to describe what you perceive. You'll start to wonder whether it's your imagination, or whether you're just delusional. And you'll eventually close your eyes again, just to fit into the world.

To me, this imaginary scenario illustrates beautifully the reasons why so many of us are struggling. We're six-sensory beings who've been conditioned to believe that we're five-sensory beings, in a world created by people who believe that they're five-sensory beings, too. Of course, the sense we've shut off isn't our eyesight but our intuition. Intuition is every bit as strong as our other senses, and every bit as real, yet we've been conditioned to treat it as our imagination if it rears its head and ignore it.

When we deny that part of ourselves—one sixth of our senses—we deny a part of who we are. And this is why empaths and highly sensitive and intuitive people struggle in this world. They are forced to deny one of their fundamental senses that helps them to navigate the world, and in doing so, they end up feeling lost and confused.

Empaths *are* different. I felt such relief when I understood this. The trick, I learned, is to realize this difference and embrace it. Over the years, with the help of my students and readers who have shared their own experiences with me, I've built a deeper understanding of the journey we're all on, especially my fellow empaths, to actually become our true selves—to stop "doing" everything we can to protect and advance the interests of the people around us, to the detriment of our own happiness. It took a very dramatic experience—my clinical death—to fully unleash my empathic abilities, but you don't have to die to learn how to harness the power of being an empath, and to protect yourself against the liabilities that come with that. On the next pages, I'll share my tools, experiences, and stories of those I've worked with, to help you step into your true self—your six-sensory, empathic, magnificent self. By the end of this book, you'll realize that being an empath is a superpower!

Quiz: Are You an Empath?

Want to see how empathic you are? Answer yes or no to the following questions, then calculate your results.

1. You fear hurting other people's feelings, disappointing them, or letting them down because you can feel their pain (possibly to a greater degree than they do).

2. You have a willingness to accept full responsibility for your actions, sometimes to the point of taking blame for something that's not your fault.

3. You can be easily manipulated by others and often feel taken advantage of or exploited.

4. You have difficulty receiving compliments, gifts, services, or kindness from others. You feel obligated to repay them immediately.

5. You're highly compassionate toward other people and tolerant of their weaknesses, insecurities, and mistakes. You treat others with kindness whether they deserve it or not.

6. You understand other people better than they understand themselves, so people often come to you with all their troubles and

issues. Even though this may weigh you down, you never turn them away because you can feel their pain.

7. You're deeply intuitive, and just know things without being told. It's a depth of knowing that goes beyond just a hunch.

8. When someone says one thing and means another, you can easily tell.

9. You're gentle on people and on the planet.

10. You're attracted to the healing arts in all its forms, including holistic therapies.

11. You tend to support the underdog and are very quick to spot that person in a group or room.

12. You have a tough time wearing pre-owned clothing because you can feel the energy of the person who owned them before you. You just don't feel like yourself in them.

13. You love daydreaming and have a deep and rich inner world. You're highly creative, a visionary, and you need the space to create.

14. You find routine, roles, and control extremely claustrophobic, and like the freedom to do your own thing in your own time.

15. You're attracted to all things metaphysical and spiritual.

16. You're very service-oriented. Helping people brings you great joy.

17. You're very interested in self-growth, self-help. You want to evolve. You want to learn. You want to grow. You not only want to evolve yourself, but you have a deep interest in evolving humanity as well and helping humankind to evolve.

18. When in certain geographical locations—a sacred spiritual site, a battleground (even unmarked), or the home of a historical figure—you sometimes feel flooded by the emotions of those who were there before you.

19. Being in nature brings you great peace and a sense of calm.

20. You have a deep affinity for plants. You just know what a plant needs—a certain nutrient, water, to be moved to a specific location—when no visible signs are apparent.

21. You sense the energy of food and know whether it will give you energy or deplete it.

22. You have a deep connection with animals. They just gravitate toward you.

23. You've always struggled with trying to fit into society or the world. You observe much of what goes on in life as though watching an ad on TV, as if these goings-on don't involve or apply to you.

24. When you're near someone who's not feeling well, you find yourself feeling their symptoms: nausea, headache, chills—doesn't matter. And often, they walk away feeling better.

25. You have difficulty relaxing when people are around you. You can't fully let yourself go. You have a need for solitude and a

space to regroup from other energies, and get aggravated if you can't have that space.

26. Crowded places, such as malls, are especially difficult for you.

27. While others may feel music needs to be loud to be experienced, to you, it feels like a full-out assault on your nerves.

28. When standing next to someone—anyone, anywhere—you sometimes mistake their thoughts for yours.

29. When talking with someone, in an effort to understand them, you find yourself lost in that person's thought process and lose track of your own.

30. You're sometimes overcome by feelings that you know aren't your own. You're walking along, minding your own business, and *wham!* You're hit by a wave of sadness, suddenly feel incredibly irritated, or even—and this is the best—a surge of joy.

31. Because you pick up on the energies that are happening to others, or even around the planet, you feel fear and anxiety easily. Often the smallest thing makes you feel fearful, anxious, overwhelmed, or stressed.

32. It's difficult for you to watch or read frightening, sad, or depressing movies or books. You can become physically ill.

33. You're easily distracted by, well, anything (because you notice everything), so it's hard to focus in a classroom, during a meeting at work, or at a party. You're never going to go to a coffee

shop to write up a report, put the final touches on your project breakdown, or churn out your blog.

34. You often feel emotionally and physically exhausted. You got eight hours sleep, have been drinking plenty of water, don't have any emotional issues that should plague you at the moment, but you just want to lie down.

Take a look at your results:

- If you answered yes to one to nine questions you definitely have partial empathic leanings. You're quite good at keeping other people's energies at bay, but you sometimes have trouble setting boundaries, so you might benefit from energy work, such as polarity therapy, qigong, shiatsu, pranic healing, and Reiki. You have fairly good intuition, particularly where it concerns areas of your own life, and you can usually sense a sticky situation before it arises. You're good at taking care of yourself but can be sensitive to certain foods, pollutants, and substances. Unlike other empaths, you're able to adapt easily in a city. All in all, your empath nature doesn't hinder you from following your life's work and desire. You are your own person, and are able to differentiate yourself from others.

- Answering yes to ten to nineteen questions means you're a moderate empath. You scored toward the middle of the scale on the overall results. You have strong intuitive skills and probably like to spend time in nature or by the water. You enjoy the city from time to time, but you like to get out into nature to restore your energy. You are pretty good at protecting your aura and energy space, but once in a while, other people's energy affects you. You might benefit from going to one or more of the types of energy workers listed above.

- Answered yes to twenty to twenty-eight? You scored pretty high on the overall results. You're most definitely an empath. You're pretty intuitive and can usually tell when people are lying. You may want to look into becoming an energy worker or healer, because this could be a natural gift for you. You prefer to be in nature and preferably around water. You particularly love to experience the healing properties of nature. You have a gift for influencing the moods, energies, atmospheres, and environments around you.

  You need to work on differentiating other people's energy from your own. You may have a tendency to mirror other people and their energy. Your score indicates that you would benefit from learning to run energy (flow energy throughout your body to release blocks); ground yourself (connect with the earth); and protect your aura (according to Merriam-Webster, "the energy field that emanates from all living beings")—all of which I discuss further in Chapter 3.

  You love to help others, rescue others, and heal the world; however, you need to slow down and give to yourself before you do so! You would benefit from an energy healing yourself.

- If you answered more than twenty-eight, you're a full-on empath. You are what I would call a mystic. You're highly intuitive and can almost always tell when people are lying. You're also a natural born healer. You have a deep love and appreciation for nature and unconsciously understand its healing effects.

You recognize the sacred expression of all beings. You are truly wise. And you have a wonderful ability to sway and change the moods, energies, atmospheres, and environments around you.

You need to learn how to recognize and differentiate other people's energy from your own. You feel the pain and suffering of the world on your shoulders and take it on as yours. Learning to use psychic/empathic meditation tools that I'll discuss later in the book—loving yourself, accessing your own inner knowing, expressing gratitude, and connecting with the cosmic web of consciousness—will help. You also have a tendency to mirror other people and their energy. This means that you give up your energetic seniority (the power over your own energy) at the whim of the world's changing winds (in other words, other people can control or influence you too much on an energy level). For example, if you're feeling happy and content and a friend is feeling down, miserable, or fearful, you allow that mood to highjack your own—you take on their fears and sadness, giving those feelings precedence over your own. You would benefit from learning to control your own energy, and create stronger boundaries, which I discuss specifically in Chapters 3 and 6, as well as throughout this book.

Whatever your results here, and wherever you fall on the sensitive/empath spectrum, as you read this book, you'll find stories, examples, meditations, and exercises to help you learn how to strengthen your intuition, your boundaries, and your empathic gifts to step into the power of who you truly are.

Meditation for Developing Your Intuition

———

This meditation takes you from a place of learning to listen to your intuition to one of trusting what it has to tell you. To review my suggested directions for these end-of-chapter meditations, please check the introduction.

> *"I allow myself to recognize the subtle voice of my intuition.*
> *Whether it comes to me through words or visions, I pay attention*
>   *to it.*
> *I pay attention to sensations in my body, such as feelings of calm,*
>   *peace, and relief.*
> *I honor these subtle thoughts, visions, sensations, and feelings, and*
>   *know they're my soul's way of communicating with me.*
> *I trust and feel safe in the knowledge that as I follow my intuition,*
>   *I'm serving my highest good."*

Chapter 2

EMPATH:
BLESSING OR CURSE?

MANTRA:
"My sensitivity is my superpower!"

B eing an empath comes with many powerful gifts, but it can also be extremely painful. If you're an empath but don't yet realize it, as I didn't for much of my life, it can be debilitating. You feel there's something wrong with you, that you're a failure and a loser when you can't please everyone, and you don't value yourself enough to get paid for doing work that you love. Even if you recognize that you're an empath, unless you know how to harness your intuitive energetic abilities, they can hold you back from fully realizing yourself because you always see "the other" as more important.

Our downfall, or our curse, is our inability to distinguish other people's needs and emotions from our own, and our need to make everyone else feel good before we can feel good ourselves. This is what draws us out of our inner sanctity and into other people's dramas, and why it feels like we carry a heavy burden on our shoulders. We also struggle, as we've seen, with trying to fit in to a world that's not geared toward us—we're six-sensory beings living in a five-sensory world.

Our blessings, or gifts, include the very sensitivity that causes us such discomfort. That sensitivity links us to the other side (more on that in Chapter 3), but also gives us a keen intuition, natural healing abilities, and the ability to love easily and make others comfortable effortlessly. In addition, empaths are often thoughtful, conscientious, caring, creative, and naturally great listeners.

In this chapter, we'll take a look at some of the key downfalls these traits bring with them, and near the end, we'll look at the beauty of this sensitivity and how it can help us embrace who we truly are.

Aversion to Criticism/Addiction to Approval

For empaths, the popular childhood quote of "Sticks and stones may break my bones, but words can never harm me" doesn't ring true. When we hear criticism, it gets blown out of proportion within us. For example, a little girl, feeling full of herself and in love with life, is told, "People would like you more if you weren't so loud." While one child might shrug that comment off as a crabby parent needing a little quiet, a more sensitive child might clam up and absorb the harsh comment as true, as a sign that she's unlikable when she's just being herself.

Negative thoughts—*I'm bad, I'm not enough, I'm not good*—echo in your mind, over and over. When others criticize me or even when I judge myself, I experience a physical reaction in my chest, belly, and head. Sometimes my heart beats faster, I feel warm, and my face flushes. Many of my readers and students say they feel this way, too. I've had people tell me they feel their blood pressure rise, their legs wobble, or even feel lightheaded or faint when they've had to deal with what they perceived as criticism.

It's no wonder we'll go out of our way to avoid any corrective or disapproving comments. Yet in doing so, we can become people-pleasers. It's important to understand that as you go out of your way to please people, you start to give your power to everyone else around you. You start to do what everyone else wants you to do, or what will gain their approval, as opposed to what your inner guidance system, your inner voice, is telling you.

We also lose power and our connection to our inner guidance system—and this is the flip side of avoiding criticism—when we become addicted to approval. See if this example rings true:

Someone tells you that you've done an amazing job, have a special talent, or possess excellent insight, and you think, *Oh my God, I'm finally worthy. I'm finally doing something right.* Then when that approval stops, you're so sensitive that you actually feel the loss in the form of physical symptoms—like the fight-or-flight reaction that causes your heart to race—and you immediately wonder, *What have I done to cause them to stop giving me approval? Maybe I'm not who I thought I was? How could I have been so positive about myself? How embarrassing that I believed I was so great!*

Sound at all familiar?

We can become a slave to the approval, a slave to that person who stopped giving us praise. We'll talk more about this throughout the book, but for now, just know this book will help you deal much more effectively with criticism and focus on your own inner guidance system.

Fast Track to Doormat-hood

Because of our people-pleasing tendencies, we're often prone to be the underdogs or the doormats of society. If you've ever apologized even though you're not at fault, pretended to agree with everyone because you just don't like disagreeing with people, are afraid of saying no, or feel responsible for how other people feel, then you know exactly what I mean. Being a doormat causes us to go to great lengths to avoid conflict, take on things we don't want to just to please others, and maintain relationships with people we just don't jibe with. These tendencies can steer us way off course of our soul's purpose, following what others might desire for us.

I was conducting a retreat when one of the participants, Wendy, stood up to share a story about the situation with her husband of thirty years. She crossed her arms over her stomach, looked cautiously around the room, and then said, "I married a narcissist. Oh, I didn't know it at the time, he was so charming, but from everything I've read, from what our couples counselor said before he refused to go back because 'she had no idea what she was talking about,' he is. I do everything I can to please him, just to keep the peace. It's like walking on eggshells. Everything's a perceived slight. When he comes in the door, my heart sinks."

She stood straighter. "The entire time we've been married, he's done nothing toward contributing to the relationship. He's always been this way. And when he was sick, and we thought he might not make it? I was there for him. I nursed him through. But a few years later, when I struggled with my own illness, he made me feel that I was being 'a pain in the butt' for being sick . . . He's hit me," she said, looking at the floor.

"Wendy," I said, "why haven't you left him?"

"I don't want to piss him off! I still have feelings for him!"

She was so invested in pleasing him that she'd completely lost herself, to the point where her needs no longer mattered to her.

I related to and empathized with Wendy's predicament, probably because of my cultural upbringing and dealings (I was born in Singapore but grew up in Hong Kong, a British colony at the time) with gender disparity (which I'll talk much more about in Chapter 10).

Both my parents were born and raised in India, so ethnically I'm Indian, and was brought up with its cultural norms. One of those norms is the custom of arranged marriages; you marry someone chosen by your parents. From my preteen years through the early 1980s, they groomed me to be what was considered a good wife. During the early '80s, I was a huge fan of Cyndi Lauper. I used to emulate her and dress like her. I'd spray my hair neon pink and purple, wear flamboyant clothes, and dance over and over to "Girls Just Want to Have Fun." This became my freedom song because it epitomized strength, power, and self-expression— everything I strove for in life. Expressing my inner Cyndi Lauper, I felt liberated and rebellious!

But Cyndi Lauper—her freedom, her unapologetic self-expression— was the antithesis of the type of young woman I was "supposed" to be. My parents, especially my dad, begged me to dress more "Indian," or at least more conservatively. And because I was an empath, I grew increasingly conflicted at a young age. I didn't want to hurt or disappoint my parents as they agonized over the possibility that I'd end up an old maid or a spinster outcast. They constantly worried about what others thought of me. I started to internalize their concerns until, eventually, the idea of disappointing them became almost as unbearable as the idea of following the path they'd laid out for me to follow.

To be clear, my parents were very loving. Their desire to see me married according to their customs wasn't cruel. They truly believed this was the most loving gesture they could make. They didn't understand that for me to adapt to these norms I'd have to dim my light, make myself small, and ignore the inner calling of my authentic self. In the same vein, I didn't realize at the time that my own empath nature made it increasingly difficult for me to say "no" to them without feeling guilty.

Trying to please my parents made it hard for me to maintain clear boundaries between what *I* wanted for my life and what they expected of me. Over time, bending to meet parental expectations expanded to include the expectations of everyone around me—my peers, my colleagues, even strangers. Eventually, it was simply the world at large: I couldn't deal with disapproval from anyone. Whether it was a teacher at school, a friend, or the clerk at the corner shop—I would do everything I could to win their approval.

As a child, I was shy and introverted. I attended a school filled primarily with British expatriates. Everyone was white except me. I was brown. Before I began classes at the school, my mother took me for my admission interview with the headmistress, an austere woman with pursed lips and a furrowed brow. Her demeanor conveyed the sense that I should consider myself lucky if she were to give me the opportunity to study in this prestigious institution, and that I would need to spend my time proving myself to be worthy of the privilege. As a sensitive child, I intuited her feelings toward me, and this set the tone for my early school life. It's perhaps no surprise that I was often bullied, since I had literally been led into a situation where I was set up to feel unworthy and undeserving, much like the proverbial lamb being led to slaughter.

As I grew into a teenager and young adult, I carried that feeling of unworthiness with me, believing that I had to work really hard for approval. So even when I was treated poorly or unfairly, instead of standing up for myself, I would be even nicer and do what I could to win the approval of those who disrespected me. Slowly but surely, my inner Cyndi Lauper was silenced and an enduring period of deep conflict set in. Whenever I tried to discuss with my dad my desires to pursue my dreams, we'd end up in an argument, so I hid those, too.

I know so many of you can relate to these stories. Here's the good news, though: You don't have to be a doormat any longer. As you shift to this new place of strength, watch out!

Tendency Toward Victimhood

Because empaths can give away our power, we're also prone to taking on a victim mentality, where we feel as though we've been mistreated by society. By everyone. While it's important to speak out if you've genuinely been victimized or abused, it's not possible to move on unless you claim control of your life and circumstances. Although some circumstances may be harder to heal and move through than others, it's still important to recognize that no one needs to stay a victim forever, and the goal always has to be to take back control over our lives, including getting professional help if necessary.

However, for some—and particularly people-pleasers and doormats—there's less incentive to move through victimhood and reclaim our lives. Our old victim stories allow us to shield ourselves from moving forward or taking risks in life. Blaming other people or circumstances protects us from being criticized for what could otherwise be perceived as our own shortcomings and failures.

For a people-pleaser, there are a lot of benefits to having a victim mentality. For example:

- People feel sorry for you and are more willing to pander to you without your having to make demands.
- You're more likely to get what you want without asking or coercing.
- Others are less likely to criticize you—and we know how much a people-pleaser hates criticism!
- It gives you an excuse not to take action.

In other words, victimhood becomes a tool for people-pleasers to get their way with others while remaining passive. The irony is that those who end up trapped in the victim's hold, and feed their victimhood, are usually people-pleasers themselves.

During one of my workshops, Sherry, who was in her early fifties, shared the story of her eighty-seven-year-old mother. From as far back as Sherry could remember, her mother had told her children and their father that she had a weak heart and wouldn't be around for very long. "We pandered to her every need, falling over ourselves to please her. We all wanted to make what time she had left enjoyable. And no one wanted to stress her and cause her heart to fail. But that "little time" kept stretching on and on. She was probably healthier than all of us together.

As a child, Sherry was rewarded for being the obedient one, which is a hallmark of a people-pleaser. "I spent my life trying to please my mother," she said. "I avoided crossing her at all costs. I was constantly afraid she'd die prematurely." Sherry shared that her siblings had eventually moved on, creating busy lives of their own, while she, who always made herself available to fulfill her mother's needs, was the one her mother consistently called on. "I envy my siblings their lives," she said. "They go on vacations whenever they want. Just take off! But I can't bear to leave. What if something happens while I'm gone?"

Sherry was also dealing with physical health challenges of her own, though she was still prioritizing her mother's needs.

I'm in no way saying that we shouldn't be there for our parents—or anyone for that matter—when they need us to care for them. However, in this case, Sherry identified a dysfunctional victimhood relationship pattern that had developed since her childhood, and this was now causing her resentment. Her mother needed to play the victim to gain attention from her family, and Sherry the people-pleaser daughter/co-victim was unable to say "no."

If this situation seems similar to something you're going through, you can break the pattern by valuing yourself more and learning to say "no," which I'll cover more later in this chapter and elsewhere in the book.

Sensory Overload

As empaths, our senses are easily overloaded, which can lead to our being reclusive. Let's start by identifying the different forms in which sensory overload can present itself. Our senses can be overwhelmed by too much work, big crowds, noise, and even, yes, simply by watching or experiencing violence in any form, real or fictional. Empaths feel it physically and emotionally. I couldn't watch *Game of Thrones* because I became physically ill, and half my audience felt the same way.

I receive letters from people all the time who tell me they find it hard to deal with watching television because of the violent or depressing subject matter, especially the news. They can't watch the news without feeling nauseated by all the harm that takes place on our beautiful planet. One woman who works for a news media company wrote that she didn't understand why she was getting sick all the time. She didn't put two and two together until she attended one of my events where I spoke about empaths and their traits. She said it was a big light bulb moment for her, because she identified with nearly all the traits of being an empath and realized that she was being exposed to high-crime stories all day, and her senses were being overloaded. Once she became aware, she started to mitigate the effects by taking frequent quiet breaks during the workday and relaxing in a hot bath when she got home from work. Soon after, she made a lateral move to the features department, and has had no problems since. She loves her job now.

It goes without saying that in these high-tech times of ours, sensory overload is just a click away. Never before in human history have we had access to such a steady stream (some might call it a deluge!) of information. Instant 24/7 news, influencers' tweets and posts, everyone's opinion on everything—we're always on call and online, assimilating information that's often titillating, disturbing, or sometimes downright horrifying. In the meantime, we're exposed to unprecedented vitriol as online debates and wars unfurl and everyone jumps into the fray, from ordinary people to presidents. As we click away countless times a day, we internalize fears and anxieties provoked by this omnipresent source of information.

Sensory overload also comes in the form of other people, particularly people who are emotionally needy or dysfunctional. When sensory overload is caused by other people, empaths often have a hard time disentangling themselves from relationships, for fear of disappointing others. This is particularly the case in situations that initially start out well but eventually tax our senses to the point of overload—prolonged caring for sick or demanding people (including loved ones who require special help), being in an abusive relationship, and dealing with an unfair boss or a toxic work environment. These situations trigger conflicting emotions that run deep, particularly when people we love are in the mix.

One reason empaths are so susceptible to sensory overload—and thus easily lose their connection to their inner self—is that sensory overload is *not* just registered in our minds. We empaths actually *feel sensory overload physically* in our bodies, even if that overload is emotional in nature. In other words, we manifest in our bodies the physical symptoms of the people around us, never mind the energy in any given environment. This happens because we're often unable to distinguish other people's emotions from our own. Imagine picking up the energy of every person's pain, hurt, sadness, joy, happiness, or grief, just because they've come into your spatial awareness—and not necessarily realizing that these emotions are not your own.

That's also why empaths so often experience sensory overload in crowded, noisy places. Empaths seem to absorb the energies of those around us into our own field, so we could certainly get drained walking through crowded cities and shopping malls. Prolonged bouts of sensory overload can leave us feeling deeply fatigued, susceptible to headaches, or even lead to more serious illnesses. That's what happened to me when I got cancer.

Now imagine internalizing the anxieties of the world that come from the torrent of stressful, often cataclysmic news streaming into our lives from social media every minute. You get the picture: You can only soak up so much of the anxiety and fear and stress generated by others in your energy field before you're unable to differentiate between their emotions and thoughts and your own, causing you to lose your own sense of identity.

Our tendency to get lost in the emotions of others contributes to our developing nonconfrontational, people-pleasing personalities, because conflict also leads to sensory overload. But avoiding conflict leads to other problems, such as neglecting our own needs for fear of being judged; keeping frustrations pent up; not being honest for fear of disappointing others; and not allowing our own authenticity to shine through—and so a cycle begins. Relationships get messed up because we don't learn how to work through conflict peacefully. It's a skill that needs to be learned, and we have to start by making friends with conflict, instead of avoiding it.

Sometimes we actually try to protect our sensitive inner natures with a tough exterior, which seemingly contradicts the nonconfrontational style of the people-pleasing empath. But don't be fooled. We protect ourselves from the onslaught of sensory overload this way—by developing unique coping mechanism tools, which I call *layers*, to block the pain. These layers create a protective shell around our sensitive, empathic selves. The more we're exposed to sensory overload, the more layers we develop or add.

These layers might include aloofness and detachment (which makes it hard to develop intimate relationships), or escapism through drinking, drugs, overeating, or gambling. The more adverse our environment, the more layers we might add to protect ourselves from the outside world.

When this happens, even the positive actions we take—like joining a 12-step program or attending intensive self-help workshops—might only add more layers. (Of course, it's important to recognize that 12-step and similar programs have positive effects on countless people who can't address their real issues until they're sober.) In other words, these layers might help us manage our addictions or help us develop stronger boundaries. They won't, however, necessarily address the root cause of our issue, which is our sensitivity to sensory overload.

The Beauty of Your Sensitivity

Now here's the dichotomy. As empaths, our connection to our higher world—the other side, the unseen realm I went to when I died, where we're all connected outside time and space—is stronger than someone's who isn't as sensitive or empathic. Our intention to follow that guidance is stronger. And that is our strength.

When you follow that higher calling, your life works out in magical ways.

It's when you give your power to the outside world that you lose your connection to your inner sense of knowing, and your life starts spiraling downward. The pain of this dichotomy—our connection to the higher calling, our higher selves, and our tendency to give our power away to those outside us—can cause empaths to turn themselves inside out to avoid any criticism or to gain approval; we'll do anything to ease the suffering. This deep awareness and calling, and the subsequent need to subvert ourselves to fit into a five-sensory world, can lead to depression, suicidal tendencies, or drug dependency as a path to escape that kind of internal pain. And who feels more internal pain than anyone? It's the empaths.

Now when I look back before my NDE, I gave that critic my power at that time. I blocked my sensitivity and it took me off my path. Empaths sometimes do try to block their sensitivity, but it's not ultimately helpful. Your sensitivity opens up your six-sensory world. It's connected to the other side. If you block your sensitivity you block what's coming in from that other realm. The thing is to be aware that you're giving your power to the outside world, and to start giving it to your own inner world or to your higher self.

Today I'm very, very conscious of turning inward and constantly tuning in. My reason for sharing what I share is because I want you to learn how to tune in to your inner selves, too. This is your salvation. This is your purpose. This is how you can really turn your lives around and do good. It's how you can fully realize the gifts that make you so caring, kind, insightful, and generous—the gifts that connect you with the other side.

I'm reminded of the famous Italian artist Michelangelo, who, when asked how he'd managed to carve such a beautiful statue of an angel from such a rough block of marble, replied, "The angel was always there. I just chipped away at the marble until I set him free." So here's something to ponder: What if your sensitive self is actually that angel inside the marble, struggling to be set free? What if the real solution to staying in touch with your inner mystic is to chip away at the layers you've accumulated—that is, the marble—and set yourself free? Wouldn't it serve us better to learn how to hone the gifts of the angel rather than layer them deeper inside the marble?

Meditation for Embracing Your Gifts

While this meditation may feel slightly awkward at first, and you may not believe yourself, keep at it.

After a time—it could be minutes, days, weeks—you'll begin to believe these words and embrace the beauty of who you truly are.

> *"I see my sensitivity as my strength and superpower.*
> *It's a part of who I am.*
> *I love and accept myself for who I am.*
> *I no longer need anyone else's approval to accept me or my sensitive*
> *nature.*
> *I no longer forsake myself nor beat myself up for being a sensitive*
> *soul.*
> *My sensitivity serves a purpose.*
> *My soul chose me to experience this for a reason.*
> *Sensitivity is a rare gem that I feel privileged to have."*

PART II

———— ∞ ————

Your Relationship with Yourself

Chapter 3

HOW TO LIVE LIFE MORE
OPTIMALLY AS AN EMPATH

MANTRA:
"I am like water, both gentle and strong."

Embracing your six-sensory self can expand your world. When you open your eyes, as we talked about in Chapter 1, everything is brighter and more intense. If you've spent years suppressing your very essence, tamping down what makes you unique, you're flooded with feelings, emotions, and insights. Allowing yourself to feel everything, and more deeply, you'll find that much of what you perceive can bring pain. But it can also bring great joy, and in that joy lies freedom.

At the same time, people have reported that when they embrace their six-sensory selves they experience more synchronicities in their life. They feel more guided. They shift from feeling small, inadequate, and viewing their empathic nature as a weakness that needs to be hidden at all costs, to embracing their nature full-on, seeing it as a gift, something unique and special, something to be proud of.

When you embrace your empathic nature, everything looks different. Your life takes on a deeper meaning. You experience a feeling of purpose. You feel such joy—a sense of coming home to who you are, and a stronger tie to the mystical world around you. Opening your eyes is absolutely worth it. But you need the tools to cope with this heightened awareness.

As I've mentioned, after my NDE and my subsequent experience with the shaman in Costa Rica, there were no tools available for me—no guidebooks, no protocols to follow. Yet I didn't want to turn off my sensitivity. That's what got me into the whole predicament with cancer in the first place—denying a part of who I was. I don't want that to happen to you. So in this chapter, I offer you my key power tools, so that, as you read the rest of this book, you'll have the foundation to open to and embrace your sensitivity, and in the process, discover your strength.

Unplugging

The outside world is loud and demanding, so the first step in honing our powers is learning to deal effectively with sensory overload. We have to identify and manage the things that jam our inner guidance system. And that involves turning the volume *down* on the outside world so we can hear what's going on *inside*.

You can start this process by making a simple commitment to turning off all your electronic devices for at least one full day—for a full twenty-four hours per week. Yes, this means turning off your TVs, cell phones, *and* computers for one day a week and only taking emergency calls. You can slowly increase this to two days a week so that, like fasting, you start to detox your system from all the noise and information that we constantly "ingest." If it's not feasible to unplug completely for one or two full days a week, you can get creative—maybe you unplug for three hours each evening and first thing in the morning. Try whatever works for you and provides relief.

Remember, social media is more problematic than other forms of media because it's omnipresent. We're literally plugged into it 24/7 through our electronic devices. A text arrives, and we feel an immediate urgency to reply, which converts to stress. Constant interruptions and distractions abound. Some people are so hyped by their smartphones that they literally risk lives by texting while driving. We internalize social media messages in regular microdoses all day long and are kept on high alert through crises that might be real or might be overstated to boost ratings, because fear sells.

I dislike the constant "breaking news" on TV for this reason. In some cases, the same level of intensity and airtime given to an earthquake, a school shooting, or a war—events that actually claim lives—is given to a tweet from a celebrity or politician. This feeling of injustice and imbalance adds to the sensory overload. Ditto for drug ads that cite side effects worse than the symptoms they're supposed to manage! The ads themselves are unhealthy and contradict their intention of well-being and health.

As Dr. Joe Dispenza suggests in his book *You Are the Placebo*, an idea that's planted in our mind, particularly if it's done repeatedly, can come to fruition.[1] So if we're bombarded with messages about illness and we're highly suggestible, it's more likely we might manifest a full-blown illness in our bodies. (I'll discuss this in more detail in Chapter 6.) If we're barraged with news about tragedies and death, it's just as likely that we'll manifest full-blown anxiety in our psyches. This is amplified countless times if you're a highly suggestible empath.

We also take to heart and internalize the vitriol and rubbish spewed by angry Internet trolls (those whose sole purpose is to argue, disrupt, distract, or post inflammatory content on the Internet) and malevolent commenters who are empowered by their online anonymity. But it's profoundly important that we empaths stay true to our empathic nature and not feel as if we have to *become* like them (the trolls) in order to *deal* with them.

I'm not suggesting that fighting sensory overload means sticking our heads in the sand. Instead, we just need to streamline our so-called "media diets" and make room for silence. It's the only way to stay in touch with our inner guidance and, in so doing, be of greater service to humanity.

Get in Touch with Your Inner Mystic

The next step in the process of empowering yourself and supercharging your gifts is to get in touch with your inner guidance, or what I call your "inner mystic." If you commit to the simple practice of plugging in to yourself, pretty soon you'll have extra space in your mind and your psyche that was once filled with stressful thoughts overloading your senses.

It's like being unaware of the noise from an air-conditioning unit until someone switches it off, and then suddenly "hearing" the silence. You'll develop a deeper connection with yourself and notice more synchronicities happening in your life. For example, you might be thinking about someone, and they'll call. Or, out of the blue, a question you've been chewing on for a while is answered by someone unknowingly. Or, you're pondering an issue, and suddenly a song comes on the radio and the words seem to hold a meaning that applies to your situation, giving you the resolution.

You'll also begin to feel more guided and have more insights. You may suddenly develop more clarity about how to deal with a difficult coworker or family member. Or, if you're an artist, your creative juices will flow more easily, opening up your channels to your art, be it music, visual arts, writing, or whatever. This is because you'll have created the space for this guidance to come into your energy field, instead of filling that space with energies that are not your own.

This state of listening to our inner voice or voices, and heightened clarity, is available to us all the time. Our busy, stressed-out, overloaded senses often prevent us from accessing this state of mind, and when we've lived like this for a number of years, it starts to feel normal. Often, we don't even realize that the fears and stresses we've taken on in our minds and bodies aren't ours. This is why it's important to have strategies that both honor and empower our sensitive natures.

Empaths often come into the world with a keen spiritual and intuitive facility. In *The Empath's Survival Guide*, Dr. Judith Orloff writes that unlike highly sensitive people, actual empaths "can sense subtle energy, which is called 'shakti' or 'prana' in Eastern healing traditions."[2] Some "have profound spiritual and intuitive experiences" and "are even able to communicate with animals, nature, and their inner guides."[3]

I most definitely have a relationship with my inner guide, as do the empaths I work with. You can call this guide your inner mystic, God, self, higher self—whatever resonates with you. I think I've had this inner voice since I was a child. As a teenager, I would hear it speaking inside my head, guiding me during the toughest times, like when I was getting bullied. *Don't be afraid of them*, the voice would say. *They're weaker than you are.* And *It may not seem that way right now, but we've got you. You are safe.* But I didn't always embrace the voice. In fact, there were times I feared it because it seemed to go against the voices coming at me from the world outside. I lost track of it for a long time.

The empath's energetic internalizing of other people's pain, be it emotional or physical, not only creates more static that further distances us from our inner mystics, it can wear us out and make us ill. In my case, it literally almost killed me. Had I learned to embrace the inner voice and heed what it was saying to me, I feel my life would have turned out very differently.

Your inner mystic is an internal guidance system that helps you weather the storms of the outside world by connecting you to Spirit and to your soul's purpose. It aligns you with the Universe in a way that transcends faith or belief, religion or dogma, which is why it's so important to honor that voice, even if it means going against what others may expect of you.

The three main reasons we suppress those voices, lose touch with our inner mystic or guides, and give our power away are: our aversion to criticism; our need for approval; and, as Matt Kahn, spiritual teacher and author of *Everything Here Is to Help You: A Loving Guide to Your Soul's Evolution*, writes, because empaths believe "we will be more *liked* by others if we are *like* others."[4] So many people write to me about these issues, people who've dealt with them all their lives.

As a child, I always felt a deep connection to the mystical, and I just seemed to sense things that I couldn't possibly know. My family dismissed everything as my imagination, but they still couldn't deny I was different. For example, when the phone would ring, I'd blurt out who was calling before anyone picked up the phone. I was always right, and I wasn't guessing—I just *knew*. This was before the days of cell phones and caller ID. Sometimes I'd hum a song and my brother would turn on the radio, and that very song would be playing in that very moment. Once, when our dad was returning from a business trip to Japan, I said to my brother, "I can't wait for Dad to get home! He's bringing surprises. He bought me a stuffed dog and a toy projector for you—from Japan!" I had no way of knowing this, but sure enough, that's exactly what he'd bought for us during his trip.

I assumed that everyone had this sort of inner voice guiding them at all times. And, indeed, I believe we *are* born with a connection to Spirit, which is evidenced by children's vivid imaginations, invisible friends, and sensitivity to the feelings and emotions of others. They seem to have an ear cocked to their inner voice. They also come up with the most amazing insights and wisdom, seemingly out of nowhere. However, as I've said, they quickly lose touch with this sense of knowing, because it gets dismissed as imagination. And they end up suppressing this sensitivity to fit in to their world.

Recently, in one of my weekly videos that I create for my Facebook Live audience, I talked about this connection to the other side, and asked my viewers to submit their own stories. The response was overwhelming.

Maria described a vivid dream she'd had about her mother, who lived across the country. In the dream, her mother was crying for help. Maria woke from the dream with a jolt. When she realized she'd dreamed her mother's cry for help, she tried going back to sleep, but found herself feeling agitated and disturbed by how real it had felt. The following morning, she got news from a family member that her mother had fallen on her way to the bathroom in the middle of the night, and had been lying on the floor crying for help. Thankfully, someone finally heard her cries and came to her rescue. It turned out she'd broken her hip. She's fine now and all is well. But while Maria's mother was lying on the floor, she'd been thinking of her daughter, and she worried that she was going to die there on the floor if no one heard her. "If anything like that happens again," Maria said, "I'm going to pay closer attention. I could have called someone to help her. Thank goodness someone did."

Cheng wrote that he'd been driving one night, and as he approached a four-way intersection, where the light was green in his favor, he started picking up speed because he wanted to catch the light before it turned red. Suddenly he heard, "*Stop!*" He had no idea where the voice came from. It wasn't loud, not even audible, yet it was jolting, sudden, and extremely clear to him. So he slammed on his brakes. And sure enough, a huge semitruck sped across the intersection right in front of his car, running a red light. Had Cheng not stopped, his fate would have been sealed.

Everyone has stories about premonitions, loved ones reaching out who are ill or have passed over, or the strong connection to the invisible world they felt as a child. Yet, many of those who shared their experiences said they couldn't talk about these things freely, for fear of being thought of as crazy.

Since time immemorial, philosophers and mystics have asserted that we come into this world knowing about the "other world" from where we came, but we soon forget. Empaths, as a group, are often in touch with this etheric realm and live with a vague longing for an "elsewhere" that we can't define. It's been my experience that those who feel this deep yearning in their hearts seem unable to stay in one place for too long. They often end up spending their lives searching for a place that doesn't exist in this physical word. They're the ones who can lose themselves while at their workplace, staring out of their window into the open skies, longing to be elsewhere. They're the children in the classroom whose minds wander, as they imagine roaming faraway lands instead of focusing on the textbook lying open on their desks. Perhaps this longing for something unnamable is what the poet William Butler Yeats meant in his poem "Before the World Was Made": "I'm looking for the face I had / Before the world was made."[5]

And that's where strengthening our connection with our inner mystic comes in. Those who are connected and listen to their inner guidance are very present in their lives. It doesn't matter what their occupation—bricklayer, postal worker, artist, healer—they seem to have a joy about life, and a sense that they're doing what they're meant to be doing. They're following their soul's calling.

Accept that your inner world is real. It's real, and you have to empower it. This guidance from our inner world is not just for a chosen few. It's not as though some cosmic guidance counsel is sitting up there saying, "Huh, are we going to pick on her? She's going to be chosen. He's going to be chosen," and forget about the rest of the people. It's available for everybody, but in order to tune in to it, you have to do the work. Our guides are sending these signals out to us all the time. And the more we tune in to them, the more they send these signals to us, and/or the more we hear. It's there all the time, but it's our choice as to how much we want to tune in, how little we want to tune in, or not to tune in at all.

In the coming pages, I'll explore how we empaths can get in touch with, embrace, and strengthen our connections to our inner mystics and truly own our unique power.

Connect with the Web of Consciousness

Once you connect with your inner mystic, you can reach out to connect with cosmic consciousness. My experience with death taught me that our natural state is one of freedom and liberation from the torment of loneliness, guilt, and other burdens that we take on during our lifetime. The more we can release or transcend these emotions that shackle us to our dramas, the more we can feel the connection to our inner mystic and to the vast cosmos that is our natural home.

In the same way that electricity is always available to us if we plug in to it (even if its force is invisible), so, too, is the intuitive wisdom of our infinite selves always available if we choose to connect to it. We can do this by working through and clearing any emotional baggage that bogs us down (more in Chapter 8). We can do this by forgiving those whom we perceive have harmed us, instead of holding on to past resentments (which doesn't mean we condone their behavior, or allow them into our lives if we don't want to). And we can connect by feeling grateful for all that is good in our lives, or anything else that elicits a feeling of lightness, relief, or liberation.

I refer to our infinite selves as our connection to pure consciousness, and I see consciousness as one giant web, connecting all of us. One of the things I learned during my NDE is that we are all connected, as though woven together in a giant web. I call this the "web of consciousness." Imagine that all of us are connected by this web, but instead of actual filaments, the threads are energy. And though you can't see it, you can intuit it. You can feel it, that energy.

Most of us aren't even aware of this web until we leave our bodies at death, but in actuality, our consciousness is always connected to all that is, which includes one another. When I was in the coma, I was without my body, but I could feel what everyone else was feeling. I could feel all their emotions, including the resignation of the doctors at my imminent fate, and the emotions of my distraught family members. Through this great web, I was connected to all of time and space, and I was aware of not only what was going on in the hospital room but beyond, including my brother flying across the continent to come and see me, as well as other lives I'd lived in various incarnations, especially those where I shared a connection with my current family members. Time and space didn't seem to exist. It felt as though I could access all of time, all at once.

We can see evidence of this web everywhere. I mentioned in the previous chapter about how my dog, Cosmo, knew I was coming home five minutes before I'd walk in the door. I believe our pets, animals in general, and our babies are aware of our connection to one another through this web. I have so many stories from people who've written to me about animals, babies, and children who know things or sense things that, using our five-sensory way of thinking, they couldn't know.

One woman, Lesley, wrote to tell me that her five-year-old son went into her bedroom in the middle of the night and said he'd just seen Grandma, who told him to tell his parents that she was okay. Lesley was puzzled, because as far as she knew, both her mother and her husband's mother were fine and in their respective homes. The following morning, she found out that her mother-in-law had passed during the night, right around the time her son had seen her.

Another woman wrote in telling me that one night her dog, who normally slept outside, had insisted on sleeping with her on her bed. She'd tried to coax him outside, but he wouldn't go, so she let him sleep with her, believing that maybe he was feeling lonely or needed extra attention. During the middle of the night, she was awakened by a phone call from her dad to tell her that her mother had passed away. Her dog was right there next to her, snuggling up to her and licking the tears off her face as she sobbed into the phone upon hearing the news. He stayed close to her for the whole night, and didn't leave her side. She was convinced her dog knew her mom was going to pass that night, and knew that she would be distraught and in need of comfort. These sensitive beings are aware of these events as strongly as you're aware of this bound book or electronic reader in your hands.

We've switched off the awareness of this connection just to be able to fit in, in the world. We've been brought up to believe that we're all separate, individual beings, so we live in a world where we compete with one another. While we live in a world where it's all about "conquer or be conquered, kill or be killed, eat or be eaten," in actuality what happens to me affects you and vice versa. We're like fingers on a hand: If you hurt one finger, the whole hand hurts. We're not individual fingers; we're all connected by the palm of that hand.

We are always connected to our spirit, whether we realize it or not. To own our emotional or spiritual power in the world we don't need to "fix" ourselves or add more layers to our lives. We don't need layers of spiritual dogma or layers of self-denial masquerading as self-improvement. As with Michelangelo finding his angel in the block of marble, we need to *strip away* these layers and chip away at the false beliefs, thought patterns, fears, and unnecessary pressures that jam our internal radar and hinder our connection to our inner mystics.

Strengthen Your Energy

Empaths have different levels of energy—partial, moderate, strong, and full-on, or mystic. But no matter the level, it's important to build your own energy practice.

Ground Yourself

Grounding yourself helps you relax, strengthen your spiritual connection, and get clear about which energies are your own and which belong to others. The more grounded you are, the more easily you can connect with your inner mystic, and the less susceptible you'll be to the energies of others.

I have a number of grounding exercises I practice. Here's one of my favorites. Feel free to change it up however you like.

1. Find a quiet place to sit where you won't be disturbed. If the weather's nice, you might want to find a patch of lawn outside to sit on. You can close your eyes or leave them open. It's totally up to you.

2. Take a deep breath in. As you're breathing in, imagine that you're breathing in life force energy (power or cosmic energy), positive life force energy, just breathing it in and filling your vessel with that life force energy. You can do it slowly.

3. Now take a deep breath out. Let it all out. Your breathing is slowing everything down, including lowering your blood pressure, slowing down your heart rate.

4. Do it once more, a deep breath in and another breath out.

5. For the third and last breath, draw a deep breath in, and just allow yourself to visualize that the breath is going even deeper, into your legs, into your feet, and in fact, you're drawing it in so deeply that the breath is coming out through the bottom of your feet and rooting itself into the ground. And then take a deep breath out.

Protect Your Aura

It's critical to protect your aura daily, especially if you're in crowds, around energy that's making you uncomfortable, or with someone, such as a narcissist, who may be depleting your energy. There are all kinds of methods, but many of them require you to shield yourself from the energy of others. While this can be very helpful for some, for empaths it goes against the grain. For our growth, we don't need to separate or hide. We need to connect, to expand rather than contract. With that in mind, here are a few quick methods I often use.

- Carry a piece of black tourmaline with you. It's well known for protecting against energies that might cause you discomfort. You can carry a stone in your pocket or find beautiful jewelry made with this crystal.

- Smudge your aura with a white sage smudge stick. Or you can achieve the similar effect by spraying sage mist. This Native American practice is especially helpful to cleanse your aura. Try it after you've been in groups of people. You can also spray witch hazel or water.

- Strengthen your aura. Sit down in a quiet place. Picture your aura—whatever color comes to you—expanding and filling the room, getting larger and larger, as far out as you want to extend it, then slowly pull it back, until it's inches from your body. Repeat this a few times. Strengthening your aura helps you expand and contract it at will, so that if you're in an environment that makes you uncomfortable, you can pull it closer to you and avoid picking up unwanted energy.

- Keep your body healthy—drink plenty of water, exercise, go outside. These practices help you clear your energy and center you.

ANITA MOORJANI

Run Your Energy

Running energy—moving energy through your body to avoid blocks, like turning the water on high to undo the kinks in a hose that are stopping the flow of water—will help you ground with the earth energy and with the divine. It will open your body's seven major centers of energy, or chakras, and balance your life force energy.

There are many exercises for running your energy. This is one of my favorites.

1. Sit quietly and close your eyes. Imagine a beautiful, bright beam of light entering through your crown from above. As it enters your crown, be aware that this is your connection to the divine. This is your divinity.

2. As it's entering through your crown, it's bathing the entire inside of your head and your throat, and going down into your chest, your arms, your abdomen, down into your buttocks, through your legs, and down to your feet. This beautiful light can take on any color that you would like it to, or any color that it chooses. It can be a rainbow of colors, or it can be pure white. It's beautiful, bright, and strong. This is your divinity. This is you.

3. See this light as being really bright, so that it actually emanates a beautiful aura that surrounds your body, a bright glow that appears around your body. The brighter the beam of light that's in your body, the larger the aura that it creates. That is your powerful life force energy.

4. Now see that light coming out through the soles of your feet and going down into the ground, all the way down into the earth in all its colors, or in whatever color you have chosen.

5. See it spread its branches in the earth, going deeper and deeper and wrapping itself around the magnetic force in the center, the core of the earth, so that you are very much part of the Earth. You belong to this earth right now. But you are connected to the divine because you are divine. You are a piece of heaven living on Earth, a piece of God, a piece of the divine living on Earth right now, being an expression of love, shining your light here.

6. Feel yourself back in this room, in this moment in time, and feel yourself back in your body again. Feel your fingers and your toes. Take a few deep breaths, then open your eyes.

Practice Inaction in Action

As empaths, we need to learn to work through conflict in a nonconfrontational way, so that we don't become conflict-avoidant. My mother taught me a way of doing this that works perfectly with my empathic nature. The *Tao Te Ching* refers to it as "*Wu Wei*," which translates roughly to "action through inaction." It's a paradox that suggests that inaction is sometimes the best form of action, but it can also be interpreted as "gentleness overpowering strength."

My mother's lesson about *Wu Wei* occurred when I was a little girl. A bunch of bullies used to stand in wait for me at the school playground during recess, and surround me. They knew that I always had these clown-shaped, sugar-frosted, brightly colored cookies, and they were after them. There were three boys, all of them taller than me. There I was, slightly chubby in my uniform gray tunic dress, thick gray wool socks pulled straight up all the way to my knees (because I thought that's how you were supposed to wear them), with my thick, dark, wavy big hair, clutching my snack bag, looking petrified. I was a walking target. One boy would tap me on my shoulder so I'd look behind me, and then another would approach me from the front and snatch the bag out of my hands while I was distracted.

Each day, my mom would pack three of these cookies she'd purchase by the bag at the grocery store. I loved how colorful they were. Each day, the boys took them. One day I told my mom what the bullies were doing. I expected her to tell me to report them to the school authorities the next day. I imagined her adding, "You need to stand up for yourself in the face of bullies!" But instead she said, "Tomorrow I'm going to pack an extra bag of cookies. When you get to school, I want you to go up to those bullies, hand them the cookies, and say, 'I know how much you like these, so here. I'd like to share these with you.'"

I wasn't convinced, but I still took the extra bag of cookies to school the next day. When I spotted the gang of bullies in the school playground, I walked cautiously over to them, with the bag of cookies in my hands, looking at the ground, wondering if my already frail self-esteem was going to be crushed yet again. The three boys were leaning against a large tree at the end of the playground. I held out the bag as I approached them slowly. They looked at me with suspicion at first, then saw the bag of cookies in my hand.

I stopped in front of them. "I'm guessing you really like these, so I brought an extra bag for you today." My mom had packed six cookies in that bag, so that they could have two each.

Their faces softened. The leader smiled and reached out for a cookie, then gave me a high five. The other kids broke out into grins and reached out for their cookies, followed by more high fives. I walked away feeling ten feet tall and victorious. I had conquered the bullies! After that day they never bothered me again. Instead, they greeted me heartily every time they saw me. My mom had been right.

That's *Wu Wei* in action—the feeble overpowering the strong. Because we empaths are confrontation-shy, we can become masters at *Wu Wei*. By cultivating this practice, we remain connected to our inner strength and guidance system while still nurturing our sensitive natures.

Meditation to Connect with the Cosmic Web of Consciousness

Unplug, find a quiet place, and repeat these words to connect with all that is.

> *"I visualize a ball of light filling my heart space.*
> *The ball of light expands until it encompasses my whole body.*
> *I watch as it continues to expand, creating a huge aura beyond the*
> *limits of my physical body.*
> *As the aura continues to expand, it creates a huge auric field*
> *around me.*
> *The field expands so that it comes into contact with the fields of*
> *others.*
> *The more we expand our energy, the more we are connected with*
> *one another, and to the great cosmic web."*

Chapter 4

TURNING UP THE DIAL
ON YOUR EGO

MANTRA:
"I love and accept all of me, and that includes my ego."

The ego really gets a bad rap. It's perceived as the archenemy of enlightenment—or at least that's how it seemed when I used to listen to spiritual gurus in my youth and read books about contemporary spirituality prior to my near-death experience. I was always told to "suppress my ego" or "overcome my ego" at all costs if I wanted to attain enlightenment. The ego was considered the nemesis of the true self. For empaths, especially, the ego is not—as we're so often taught—the nemesis to the true self. It's the key.

You may be recoiling at that thought, but bear with me. For starters, when spiritual teachers suggest that "the ego is your enemy," an important question comes to mind: Do we even have a consensus about what the word "ego" really means? Shouldn't the definition of that word be universally understood if blanket statements are made about it?

Let's take a look at some common dictionary definitions of "ego":

Cambridge Dictionary: Your idea or opinion of yourself, especially your feeling of your own importance and ability.

Oxford English Dictionary: A person's sense of self-esteem or self-importance. Synonyms: Self-esteem, self-importance, self-worth, self-respect, self-image, self-confidence.

This is pretty much my understanding of the ego. I'm on board with spiritual teachers who are trying to communicate messages like "Don't be a brat" or "It's not good to brag" or "Humility is a good thing." I also support common spiritual messages that remind us not to mistake our false sense of self, which is influenced by the material world, with our true, authentic self. These messages are all well and good.

But the word "ego" is often used in a derogatory way, so we end up squashing our self-esteem, thinking, "I have to suppress my ego."

Freud initially put the word "ego" on our cultural map, along with the concept of the "super ego" and the "id." Over the years, psychoanalytical interpretations of the term have ended up equating the ego with narcissism, quite likely because spiritual leaders have spun it this way. That said, a humble and kind person can actually have a strong ego. The characteristics aren't mutually exclusive.

Let me explain. Each of us has an ego. In and of itself, the ego isn't a bad thing. It anchors you to your sense of self. A healthy ego protects and fortifies you. It's also important to note that there's a difference between having an ego and being egocentric. Having an ego gives you self-confidence. It gives you the strength and insight to stand up for yourself in situations where you feel vulnerable or exploited. Being egocentric, on the other hand, involves being self-centered and self-serving, often to the detriment of others. Egocentric people frequently display a lack of empathy for the needs and feelings of others and the world at large. As a result, the ego and egocentricity are often put in the same basket.

Ego and Conscious Awareness

But what if the ego isn't the problem? What if the real problem is actually a *lack of conscious awareness* of the world, the needs of others, and even oneself? To explore this, I'll borrow an analogy from my previous book, *What If This Is Heaven?* Only in this chapter, I'm going to take that analogy and gear it toward empaths. Imagine that you hold a remote control with two knobs that resemble volume dials on an old-fashioned radio. But instead of volume, one of the dials is marked "conscious awareness." The other one is marked "ego."[1]

People who have their conscious awareness knob dialed all the way down and their ego knob dialed all the way up are often what we call "egocentric." They are pure ego with no (or very little) awareness of others. Pushed to an extreme, these people can become narcissists, with a grandiose sense of self, a lack of empathy for others, and a constant need for admiration. Naturally, when an egocentric person's conscious awareness dial is turned way down, they have no awareness of their inner mystic, their higher self, or anything greater than their physical selves.

However, I believe that egocentric people don't necessarily need to suppress their egos; rather, they need to cultivate empathy and be encouraged to develop their conscious awareness. It's not possible to be egocentric when we're connected to our higher selves.

Turning the conscious awareness knob to high heightens our awareness of ourselves, our inner mystics, and the Universe. It also aligns us with our soul's purpose and brings meaning to our lives. The higher this conscious awareness knob is turned up, the more clearly we hear our inner mystic guiding us, reminding us who we truly are, where we came from, and why we're here on Earth. This heightened awareness also makes us extremely sensitive to the physical world around us and its inhabitants, to the suffering of others, for example, or the impact our actions have on others.

Most empaths naturally have this awareness knob turned up to high. This is what makes us empaths. We are innately connected to our inner mystic, as well as to the world around us. So if our ego is suppressed—if our ego knob is turned way down—we suppress our self-worth, our individuality, and our self-esteem. We end up feeling unworthy of attracting or receiving positive things, including love. All the while, we're absorbing everyone else's feelings and emotions.

When my ego was repressed, I used to beat myself up for merely *thinking* that being around certain people was draining my energy. I would say to myself, *Who do you think you are?* It really does take a strong ego to take great care of yourself and your well-being when you're an empath. For empaths, a repressed ego leaves us unable to differentiate between our own feelings and emotions and those of others. The ego is what defines our individuality, as a separate being from everyone else. And while we're all connected, some differentiation is necessary to survive in this physical world. An ego isn't needed on the other side, because we're all Spirit there, and there's no negativity or duplicity or competition.

Now when our ego knob is turned up high, working *in tandem* with our conscious awareness knob, the ego becomes a beneficial tool because it helps us identify with, and connect to, our own individuality. It allows us to differentiate our own being, emotions, feelings, needs, and desires from those of others, clarifying who we are in contrast to the external world.

If you feel yourself lost in the pain and emotions of the world around you, it means your ego knob (your sense of self) is turned way down. This still happens to me from time to time, but I've developed a few shortcuts to turn that knob back up. One way is to look at yourself in the mirror and look into your own eyes. Really see yourself through them. Tell yourself that you're safe, you're strong, you have a purpose, and it's part of your purpose to be yourself, as an individual being. Deep down, we empaths know more than anyone that we're all connected, which is why it's so hard for us to hold on to our individuality, more so than others. This is why it's important for empaths to know that it's truly okay to embrace our ego.

After all, we are the only ones with access to the very deepest part of our selves, the part of us that truly knows who we are and what we need to function at our best.

The ego is like a muscle that, when developed, helps us create filters and boundaries. It gives us a healthy sense of self-worth. The more empathic a person is, the higher their conscious awareness dial is naturally turned up. But if their ego dial isn't also turned up high, they risk losing their sense of self or diminishing themselves as they absorb the emotions and energies of everyone around them. That's why an empath's conscious awareness dial should always be operating at full force *in conjunction with* the ego dial.

Valuing the Ego

As I mentioned earlier, energetically internalizing other people's pain and emotions, or otherwise diminishing oneself in the service of others to the *detriment* of oneself, ultimately leads to physical pain or illness. In his book *When the Body Says No: Exploring the Stress-Disease Connection,* renowned expert on the mind-body connection Gabor Maté, MD, writes, "Emotional experiences are translated into potentially damaging biological events when human beings are prevented from learning how to express their feelings effectively." [2]

A strong, healthy ego protects you against this sort of well-intentioned but unhealthy state of being.

I learned this in many ways, and sometimes these experiences were dramatic. One day in 2001, my best friend, Soni, was diagnosed with an aggressive form of terminal cancer, from which she eventually died. Her diagnosis knocked the wind out of me. It was almost as if I'd been given the same diagnosis. I had grown up with this friend and known her my entire life. She had young children when the diagnosis came. I felt not only awful and literally sick to my stomach upon hearing the news, I also felt guilty. To be precise, I felt guilty for being healthy while she was sick. I felt guilty that she had small children who would suffer. I felt guilty if I went out with mutual friends while she was receiving treatment in the hospital because she couldn't be with us. Any act of self-care while my friend and her family were going through their crisis felt selfish to me. In short, I couldn't do anything good for myself without feeling guilty. So I spent as much time as possible with her, either in the hospital or at her home, helping her and playing with her kids.

I didn't realize it at the time, but sensory overload from feeling her illness in my own body was making me weaker and sicker. I wasn't listening to my inner self. My ego was so underdeveloped that I ignored all my own needs.

Then one day, about a year after her diagnosis, I felt a little lump on the left side of my neck. I went to the doctor, got a biopsy, and found out that I had lymphoma. Somewhere within the depths of fear I experienced from the diagnosis, a tiny voice inside me said, *Ahh, now you have an excuse to take care of yourself!*

As my best friend's health continued to deteriorate, so did mine. But even while I was dealing with my own illness, I was still more concerned about how everyone else around me was feeling, including my best friend, than I was about my own needs. In the end, it took a near-death experience for me to understand the importance of embracing my ego.

Had I developed a healthy ego, I would have had a more balanced relationship with my own self-worth. I would have realized that not only is it important to stay healthy, but also, actually thriving is necessary if I want to be of support to others. In other words, no amount of guilt I feel is going to help make anyone less sick, and the best and most selfless thing I can do for others is to get myself so strong that I can be of more support. If I knew then what I know now, I would have realized that my own well-being uplifts those around me and would have done whatever I could to uplift myself. I would have rested more, taken more time out for myself, connected with nature, indulged in self-care such as massages, or even going out and seeing friends. I would have done this knowing that I would then be bringing my best self to see my friend. I would also trust that my friend would want this for me, because if I sacrificed my own life out of guilt because she was sick, I risked making her feel guilty, too, adding to her burden.

I've received an outpouring from my readers and viewers sharing their success stories of how their lives have changed since they stopped turning their ego into an enemy. In one of my workshops, Amy shared that she was brought up to believe it was selfish and egotistical to put her needs first, most especially when others needed care. Because of her belief, and because she was the type of person who would be there for anyone, Amy attracted a lot of people who were extremely needy. "I don't know," she said, "I can't bear to disappoint anyone or let anyone down. It's like people sense that I'm a pushover and just flock to me." She also never really spoke up about her feelings of guilt or wanting to take time for herself. "I can't do it," she said. "When I start to say something, my throat closes up. People will just think it's my ego talking, that I want attention. When I feel the need to talk, I shove those feelings down."

Then one day, she watched one of my videos where I spoke about the ego and how important it is to embrace it. Something clicked within her, and she decided to try accepting her ego, not judging it. She started to become alert about how empathic she was to the needs of others (that was her high-conscious awareness, her inner mystic), while denying her own needs (that was her low or suppressed ego). This awareness allowed her to see more clearly how she was fulfilling the needs of others at the cost of her own. Amy understood why she so often felt tired and drained, and seemed to catch every illness going around. She then started to consciously listen to her own needs and took the time to recharge her batteries.

Much like your smartphone, when you're drained, you've expended more energy than you have available, so it's time to charge your batteries.

And empaths tend to drain our energies by trying to fulfill the emotional needs of everyone around us. It's important to be aware of your tendency to do this. It's also important to identify the trigger points that cause these energy leaks, primarily our inability to say no and our fear of conflict. As we become aware of our tendency to do this, we can place more importance on charging our batteries. If you're an empath and have a tendency to become drained, I suggest you make a list of all the things that charge your batteries. Refer to the list whenever you're feeling depleted, and choose something that will recharge you.

To further understand how important it is to recharge your batteries, imagine that we are *beings of light*. When you were born, you were full of bright, shining light, which was your strong connection to the divine. Now imagine that for your light to stay bright—to keep your energy going—you need to keep charging your battery, much in the way you charge a cell phone.

So how do you charge your batteries to keep your light shining? The first step is actually quite simple: You do things every day that nourish and feed your soul, in whatever way is meaningful for you. You might spend time by the ocean, meditate, walk in nature, listen to music, write, paint, or spend time with friends and loved ones. You might even do something as pedestrian as shoe shopping or eating pizza with your kids. It's not *what* you do—it's what that activity *does for you*. Everything that nourishes your soul and recharges your light is a spiritual activity.

Amy charged her batteries by spending more time doing some of the things she enjoyed, like reading a good book, soaking in a tub, going for a walk, or watching a movie she'd been meaning to watch. When she felt the guilt rising up within her, she would tell herself that she was recharging so that she could be a better version of herself, especially if her aim was to help others. Amy said she felt extremely empowered by this new practice of accepting her ego. She felt more energized, and no longer drained, exhausted, or susceptible to illness. She was able to really focus her energy where she felt she wanted to, and where it was most needed.

A Healthy Ego = Healthy Self-Esteem

A healthy ego doesn't prevent you from feeling sensory overload, but it *does* give you the necessary internal support to honor your needs so that you don't require an excuse, such as an actual illness, to care for your own well-being. It gives you the courage and foresight to remove yourself from a situation that's detrimental to your emotional or physical health. On the other hand, an undeveloped ego simply ensures that you'll feel everyone's pain while simultaneously feeling selfish for alleviating your own. It will keep you feeling trapped until something like an illness, traumatic event, or another life-changing occurrence comes along to rescue your emotions.

Think about it. If you feel the emotions of others very strongly—as strongly as your own (conscious awareness dial turned way up)—but you have a weak sense of self-identity, low self-esteem, or an inferiority complex (ego dial turned down to zero), then you have all the makings of a people-pleaser or a doormat. Everyone else's feelings and emotions matter more to you than your own because you're not important to yourself. You're more susceptible to being bullied and exploited. This makes you feel small and unable to say "no" when you want to. You lose yourself, your identity, and your personal power trying to please everyone else.

I call this the condition of being a "downtrodden empath," and I know it well because I *was* one. To make matters worse, instead of being encouraged to develop a stronger sense of self, I was surrounded by spiritual people and teachers who promoted the idea that the ego was not only the enemy of enlightenment and spirituality, it had to be suppressed.

To be truly healthy spiritually and emotionally, we need *both* our dials turned way up. I, and thousands of those I work with, who had our ego dials turned way down, exhibited some or all of the following traits.

Lacking in Self-Love

If your ego dial is turned down, it's extremely difficult to love yourself. (We'll go into more detail about self-love in the next chapter.) That's because the ego is the part of us that recognizes our individuality and our needs. Turning up the ego dial allows us to take care of ourselves and fulfill our needs, so that we can become a better version of ourselves.

Inauthentic

When you believe you're not good enough, you don't allow yourself to be spontaneous because you don't trust yourself. You second-guess yourself and overthink before taking action. You lose your spontaneity and your joie de vivre. You lose your *self*.

Joan, who spoke up at one of my events, always sought the approval of others, and didn't even realize how much she depended on this approval. As a result, she'd bend herself into whatever shape people needed her to be, just to ensure that she wasn't disappointing others. She was a master of backtracking and changing her opinions if she sensed the slightest disapproval in those she was talking to. At work, when she knew in her heart she'd nailed a presentation or report, she never quite believed it until someone told her. And if she felt the slightest hesitancy in someone's comments, she instantly dove into self-doubt. In her constant need for approval, she would lose herself without even realizing it. She was living a life that was inauthentic, that wasn't her own, a life based on what she thought was expected of her.

During my talk, it became clear to her that as long as she didn't live her own life, she wouldn't be able to find her purpose. In that moment, she made a commitment to herself to embrace her ego, get to know herself better, be more authentic, and win her own approval instead of the approval of others.

While it might be uncomfortable at first, imagine how that would feel! Throughout the day, just let yourself feel that freedom, until it starts to feel natural. Doing so, along with the other processes outlined in this book, will put you well on your way to being and expressing who you truly are.

Disempowered

The characteristics of a repressed (meaning inhibited, restrained, smothered) ego, which leads to low self-esteem and self-worth, include:

- A reluctance to take care of yourself.
- Treating others better than you treat yourself.
- A reluctance to be seen or heard.
- Valuing others' opinions over your own.
- Resistant to taking on challenges for fear of failing.
- Fear of disapproval.
- Being highly critical of yourself.
- Feeling unworthy of receiving compliments or gifts, or anything good, for that matter.

In extreme cases, a weak ego can lead to depression, addictions, and eating disorders.[3,4] If you have a repressed ego *and* are an empath, you'll not only absorb other people's dramas, issues, and fears, but you'll subvert your own needs to theirs. For example, let's say you have a repressed ego and have just heard that your friend has been evicted from her home. Of course you would run out and help her—that's what friends do. But now imagine that you have issues of your own—financial, health, relationship, whatever they might be—that are far greater than hers. As someone with a repressed ego, you'll put all your needs aside and see her eviction as more important than any of your own, perhaps more pressing, needs. Even as you watch your own situation becoming more dire, you'll focus your attention on helping her with her situation.

Now, let's say you not only have a repressed ego, but you're an empath to boot, and your friend calls you to say she's been evicted. As you reach out to help her, you'll feel all the emotions she's feeling as though they're your own. So on top of your own stress, your body will take on her stresses and fears, and you'll have difficulty differentiating between her emotions and yours. This is why, if you're an empath, it's so important to realize your strengths and challenges, so you're aware of how helping others at the expense of your own needs affects you.

As a doormat, I didn't feel empowered because I believed that everyone else knew more than I did, or that they were more important and better qualified than I was in decision-making—even when it came to dealing with my *own* issues! I always gave my power away to authorities and gurus, unaware that I had access to that power within myself. In addition, as an empath, I also used to take on the emotions and stresses of those around me and allowed myself to get involved in all their dramas and issues. Death taught me that no one has more authority over my own life than I do.

Let me say again that you don't have to die to achieve this awareness, and I would like to suggest a simple solution. First, if you're currently making everyone more important than yourself, be aware that you're inadvertently inviting people to have authority over your life. This awareness alone will help you consciously be more discerning about inviting those in who are more than willing to take advantage. Second, become aware of the difference between being aggressive and being assertive. Dr. Edith Eva Eger, Auschwitz survivor, psychologist, and author of *The Choice: Embrace the Possible*, nailed that difference with these words: "To be passive is to let others decide for you; to be aggressive is to decide for others. To be assertive is to decide for yourself."[5]

While it's common for people to confuse assertiveness with aggression, in my experience, doormats especially tend to believe we're being aggressive when we're actually only being assertive. Remember, you're not the one telling *others* what to do. You're only asserting what *you* would rather do. Once you get this point clear in your mind, you'll feel a huge shift.

Finally, find some gentle language that helps you assert your power. For example, "Thank you for your interest in my situation, but I'd really prefer to handle it this way" or "I appreciate your concern, but I feel more empowered when I do it that way." You get the picture.

Unable to Receive

These days, when I do workshops and ask my audience to raise their hands if they're an empath, I then ask them to keep their hands up if they feel they're really good at giving of themselves but have trouble receiving. Without fail, every empath's hand remains raised. As I've mentioned, trouble receiving is a common denominator among empaths, and especially doormats.

I was very good at giving of myself to the point of becoming drained, but I was terrible at receiving. The minute someone gave me something, I immediately felt weighed down by the feeling that I had to somehow return the favor. I didn't feel worthy of simply accepting the gift or abundance that was being presented to me. Imagine if every time you gave someone a gift, they felt it was a burden. You would feel awful. You really have to open up to receiving. It's dishonest to give and give just because you want to score karma points or because you spiritually believe it's better to give than to receive. You need for the giving to come from a feeling of fulfillment. It's so much better that way.

When you allow yourself to receive, you're turning up your ego dial, and when you allow yourself to give, you're turning up your conscious awareness dial. When both dials are turned all the way up, you can give (and receive) continuously without ever feeling tired or guilty.

Financial Scarcity

Empaths with their ego dial turned way down also have trouble earning money and being successful for a myriad of reasons, including the inability to feel worthy or deserving of abundance. This issue affected me when I was trying to be an entrepreneur and run my own business. I found myself working for my clients as well as for my employees! I couldn't be firm with my employees when they were slack in their work or about their schedules. I always found myself understanding their situation and getting sucked into their dramas, taking on their energies and their problems as if they were my own—but I still had to be there for my clients.

I also found it hard to ask for what I was worth, and always undersold myself because I believed it was egotistical to talk about my positive qualities and my strengths. I also was extremely modest on my résumés and always downplayed my qualifications, again because it felt egotistical to speak about my own success stories or my proven track record. This meant that I was always underpaid for work I was extremely experienced or qualified to do.

I often provided services for free for those who couldn't afford them, because I found it hard to say no or even to work out a barter system. Extra work for no money caused resentment from my team, so I took that on myself, to keep them from being involved.

When I shared this information in one of my workshops, I asked for a show of hands from those who related, and nearly everyone who had previously identified as a doormat put their hand up. I asked some to share their own stories. One man said his dad had always taught him not to brag about himself or his accomplishments or be boastful—in other words, don't tell people, show them. So he downplayed his accomplishments on his résumé. More often than not, he found he was more qualified to do the job than the bosses he worked for, while they were getting paid far more than he was. He grew resentful, and finally, growing sick of his resentment, found a way to discuss his accomplishments without being obnoxious about it. At first, it was difficult for him. He expected people to jump up, point their finger, and accuse him of being full of himself. But that didn't happen. As it turned out, people had no idea of all he'd done and began to see him in a new light.

Can't Say "No"

Empaths who are in the doormat phase say "no" or sometimes say "yes" simply because they don't want to disappoint people. I certainly did. This is actually dishonest. How would you feel if you realized that everyone who helped you and said "yes" only did so because they were unable to say "no"? Wouldn't you much prefer someone saying "no" instead of doing something for you that they didn't want to do? I know I would. (See more about the yes/no dilemma in Chapter 9.)

Feel Undeserving of Success

Empaths with their ego dials on low struggle with success or being successful. In my case, I didn't feel that I was deserving of success, and felt guilty when I would become more successful than others around me, especially close friends. So I either kept my successes to myself or downplayed them. Instead of seeing success as a way to help others more, doormats will typically "play small" and hide their talents and traits, for fear of being seen as greedy or egotistical.

One empath I spoke to said, "I feel ashamed that I earn more money than I need. I play it down, and don't buy expensive things because I don't want to draw attention to it. I don't want people to think I'm egotistical, or a show-off!" Of all the empaths I work with and hear from, at least 80 percent report making themselves small and asking for very little, to avoid the dreaded "egotistical" label. To them, the label sparks a sense of shame.

Shy Away from Leadership

I had trouble taking on leadership roles, as most empaths do. We don't want to draw attention to ourselves and often think we don't deserve that attention because it's "egotistical" to want it. Sadly, those who shirk their egos tend to be the wiser ones among us, the ones who are super-empathic, sensitive, strong, who have really good—yet often very different—ideas. These people aren't really interested in public attention or acknowledgment and are often extremely in tune with their inner mystic. And as I've said, as a society, we would benefit the *most* hearing from these people.

Unfortunately, some of our leaders have their ego dials turned way up and their conscious awareness dials turned way down. This imbues them with the brashness to move forward without any compassion, self-reflection, self-doubt, or awareness of others. They're able to single-mindedly focus on their goals without the discernment or awareness necessary to filter themselves, and easily manipulate the doormats, people-pleasers, and empaths among us.

Developing a Healthy Ego

I learned from my NDE that the ego serves a huge purpose. I needed it to help me embrace my individuality and my uniqueness. It helped me love myself, trust my inner mystic, and not let naysayers convince me that everything I experienced was "woo-woo" or "out there." It also offset my tendency to second-guess myself or give my power away—two key life lessons.

To help people develop a healthy ego, I ask them this question: "If you didn't have to consider the opinions of others, who would you be, and what would you be doing that makes you happy?" A weak ego causes us to worry more about other people's opinions of us than about our own needs and happiness. But when we identify what we would be doing if we didn't worry about the opinions of others, and we slowly start doing these things, it sets us free. It also makes us less judgmental toward others who have chosen to follow their heart despite disapproval from those around them.

Examples of answers I've received and some of the changes you might make if you weren't worried about the opinions of others include:

- Quitting a well-paid and secure job that you don't enjoy to pursue something satisfying but unstable.
- Allowing yourself to fall in love again after grieving the loss of a loved one.
- Coming out of the closet and allowing the world to see who you really are.
- Leaving a difficult marriage that you've stayed in for appearance's sake.
- Downsizing your home that's far too big and expensive for you, which you've been maintaining to keep up appearances.
- Dressing for comfort instead of purely for style (although it's possible to do both), for example, unapologetically exchanging those stilettos for sneakers when you've secretly been longing to do that.

Following your own heart without constantly worrying about the opinions of others helps to strengthen your ego.

Now that you understand the importance of a healthy ego, you can be compassionate without feeling sorry or guilty. You'll be empowered to *everyone's* benefit, not just your own, because a strong, confident person is more effective at uplifting others than a downtrodden doormat.

Meditation for Turning Up Your Ego

I recite these words when I need to strengthen my ego, to feel large instead of small, to expand and feel safe to express all that I am. I invite you to do the same.

> *"As I focus on my heart area, I imagine my awareness and ego knobs turned all the way up.*
>
> *With both knobs on high, I can feel my energy expand, filling me with strength, vibrancy, possibilities, and joy.*
>
> *This is my life force energy, and I always have access to it. It is my birthright.*
>
> *This energy is as powerful as I want it to be.*
>
> *With this expanded energy, I know that I am safe and can express myself.*
>
> *I feel safe to be all that I can be, to be powerful, and to shine my light as brightly as I can.*
>
> *I love myself, every part of me, including my ego."*

Chapter 5

BEING SPIRITUAL MEANS
BEING YOURSELF

MANTRA:
"Being an empath is a gift. It's my connection to all that is!"

mpaths straddle two realms: the outer world, with its fear-based messages, and our inner world, which connects us to our heart and soul. Because of our heightened sensitivity and connection, we're drawn to spiritual teachings like moths to a flame. Supportive spiritual communities make empaths—so prone to feeling different—feel that they belong, like they've come home. But often it's at the expense of listening to and following our own inner mystic.

If you're an empath with a compromised or weak ego—*and* have a people-pleasing streak to boot—then many conventional spiritual teachings can keep you floundering in doormat-hood by speaking directly to your weaknesses (your fears), rather than empowering you from within to trust *your own* inner guidance system. A healthier ego helps us immerse ourselves in the spiritual world we're so drawn to without losing or turning our back on ourselves. This chapter focuses on how the strength of self-love, trust, and faith helps us develop our spiritual connection without losing ourselves.

When I was in my twenties, not long after I ran away from my arranged marriage (more about that in Chapter 10), my parents were invited to meet a revered guru from India at a friend's home. They decided to take me with them to get his advice about how to deal with me. Why was it so difficult for me to marry and settle down? Why couldn't I conform to social norms? What was written in my stars? I, too, was hoping this guru would have some answers, because I could feel I was becoming a source of consternation for my parents about this. And I, too, was curious as to what lay in wait in my future, and what this guru had to say. After all, I'd been listening to, and believing in, various gurus throughout my life.

Once we reached the opulent home of the family who was hosting the guru, I noticed that people were mostly dressed in traditional Indian clothes and had covered their heads out of respect for him. I hadn't thought things through. I was wearing my usual jeans, a floral summery blouse, and a trendy pair of loafers, which I had left outside the house as custom dictated.

The guru sat cross-legged in an overstuffed armchair in the center of the huge living room, surrounded by at least seventy people sitting on the plush carpet. An altar was set up on a small table by his side. On the altar fragrant, rose-scented incense burned and a small plate of fruit and coconut sat as an offering to the gods. One by one, people came forward, sat on the floor directly in front of him, bowed their heads, and waited hopefully. The guru paused and pondered, then offered his blessings by placing his hands on their bowed heads as he bestowed a few kind words of advice.

Banned from Nirvana

When it was my turn, my parents gently pushed me ahead, gestured for me to sit down in front of the guru, and then sat on either side of me.

"Our daughter is already twenty-six and she is still not married," my father said in our native Sindhi language. "Can you tell us when this will happen for her, and why it is taking so long?"

I could feel myself blushing as he said this, wondering whether the guru thought less of me for still being single.

My dad then went on to briefly mention that I'd run away from an arranged marriage, trying to skim over it lightly. I could feel his embarrassment as he revisited that painful moment. The guru raised his eyebrows as my father spoke. Then he opened his eyes wide and took a long look at me. I was so anxious, I could hear my own heart beating. Was he seeing something scary, like maybe that marriage wasn't in my future? Was I going to be an old maid?

After what seemed an eternity, he finally spoke. He said I was spoiled and wasn't honoring my native culture. (Being dressed in Western attire certainly didn't help, but I hadn't been warned.) He added that I needed to change my act if I wanted to get married and went on at length about how I needed to be more subservient, respectful, and traditional. And he emphasized that men would not find me desirable because I was too independent (their families wouldn't want such a brazen daughter-in-law), implying that I would be more valuable as a person if I were married.

But the one statement that hit me the hardest was this: "You are flawed," followed by, "Until you change, you will not only *not* get married. You will also *not* be able to attain Nirvana when you reach the end of your life. That's because you will not be creating positive karma, so you will need to keep coming back until you have cleansed this pattern!"

Those words not only took me by surprise, but hit me deeply in my core, and I couldn't let them go—not then, and not for many years to come. I had grown up in a multicultural environment and had friends from all over the world. We dressed the same and shared the same ideals and values. If I was flawed, then weren't we *all* flawed? If so, how could that be? We were cultural hybrids. Our countries of ethnicity were not those of Hong Kong, where we all lived. Furthermore, we were being shaped in the educational system and pop culture of a third country (the United Kingdom), since Hong Kong was a British colony at that time. And here I was, standing in front of a guru in Hong Kong, who himself had just flown in from India. At the time, I didn't realize that I was in a very unique situation, at a unique point in space and time, and that this guru probably didn't even know what to make of me. I was obviously a misfit in his eyes.

"But how can I be denied Nirvana or create bad karma just for being who I am?" I asked somewhat timidly, wondering if the question alone made me a badass. I mean, he hadn't even *seen* my Cyndi Lauper side!

"Why would God allow you to pass into the higher realms unless you were perfect and cleansed from all negative karma?" he replied. "You would not allow someone into your home if you did not approve of them or if they were covered in mud. You need to cleanse yourself and make yourself pure of all earthly desires before you are worthy of entering the other realm to attain Nirvana."

Cleanse myself of what? What threw me was that while I believed in reincarnation and karma, I had a few questions: What part of me was flawed or impure? What part of me was causing negative karma for my future? Was I flawed because I wasn't willing to accept an arranged marriage? Was the guru referring to my dreams of traveling the world, and my longing to do so? Was he referring to my inner voice? Was he referring to the part of me that felt connected to the Universe, to something bigger than myself—and that might have transcended the guru himself? Did I need to trust and obey people like him (those self-proclaimed masters with direct access to the divine) instead of following my own inner voice?

I had so many questions but only knew one thing for sure: that single visit to see the guru was the start of my downfall. After that, I did every-thing possible to prove myself worthy and ensure my place in Nirvana.

As I write this, I'm reminded of my childhood friend, Aisha, who was single well into her late thirties, which worried her parents tremendously. Her parents were constantly taking her to see self-proclaimed masters (gurus), to ask them why their daughter wasn't yet married. Each guru had the same response. It was her bad karma from previous lifetimes. And each guru prescribed a different antidote to erase that negative karma, including burning incense every day before dawn while praying for a good husband; fasting for ten days at a time each month; refraining from bathing on the full moon; wearing white on the full moon; chanting man-tras for hours per day; spending time at the feet of the guru at the temple; going to the temple at dawn every morning to bathe the idols in milk; and my personal favorite (not!), washing the feet of said guru in milk and then drinking that milk because, supposedly, it was infused with the guru's divine energy! When I heard that one—over coffee with Aisha to catch up on her life—I almost spat out my cappuccino in disgust, which probably makes me a bad Hindu.

When Aisha eventually got married, it was to a man who was verbally abusive toward her. She accepted the proposal because she was desperate and couldn't continue to disappoint her parents. After she bore three children, her marriage fell apart. She's not sorry she got married, because she has three beautiful children, but it certainly wasn't the marriage she'd been holding out for.

Taking the Wrong Road to Paradise

I'm sure the guru meant well and believed he was being of service. He wanted me to have good karma, and from his cultural perspective, he be-lieved his advice would lead me in the right direction. But from that point on, I started to mistrust myself and suppress my inner voice. (Why would it compel me to do things that contradicted our cultural norms and the world at large around me? Did following my heart mean veering off course?) I started to believe that heeding the call of my inner voice would actually lead me *away* from heaven—and possibly toward hell. I tried to be "more spiritual" and "purer," throwing myself into spiritual practices to create positive karma and someday transcend from this realm into Nirvana. I meditated, prayed, chanted, attended many spiritual classes and teachings, and studied various spiritual books. Although in and of itself, there's nothing wrong with that, I was just trying too hard to *get it right.*

Certain messages in these teachings came up time and time again:

- We must be of service to humankind.
- We must forgive those who have hurt us.
- It's better to give than to receive.
- We must love our enemies.
- We must suppress our egos.
- Even those who have hurt us are our teachers.
- We must look for the lesson in adversity.

Some of these messages had conflicting counter-messages. For example, some spiritual practices are predicated on the idea of renouncing the material world, in the context that money is bad. But others advocate the idea of manifesting abundance, even if that means manifesting the means to buy a fancy new sports car or a fleet of Learjets.

As empaths, acquiring tools to strengthen our inner connection is balm for our souls. Most empaths I know, including myself, love activities like group meditations and chanting, and learning tools such as energy clearing, chakra balancing, and other balancing and healing modalities. I threw myself into all these activities and lessons with gusto. All of them. At once. The more activities I took part in, the more spiritual I was or would become. If I didn't do them, I'd prove myself unworthy, less spiritual. I took the words of spiritual teachers as gospel. I started to give and give of myself, never allowing myself to receive because I felt it was unspiritual. I volunteered my services at ashrams, orphanages, soup kitchens, and homeless shelters, which is not a bad thing to do. But I would continue to serve even when I was tired and had no more to give. I still gave, to accumulate good karma.

In situations where I'd been hurt or bullied by people, I turned the other cheek and told myself I had to unconditionally forgive and love those who'd hurt me, despite the deep pain I'd experienced. I would judge myself for feeling resentment, anger, or any other "unspiritual" emotions while they continued to hurt me. The big message to myself? I needed to forgive them and learn to love them unconditionally, but I didn't realize that I had to learn to love *myself* first.

Before I delve into the healing power of self-love, let me describe what happens when we misconstrue spiritual messages in ways that actually *diminish* our spiritual currency. In my case, I allowed people who had hurt me to continue walking all over me, while I tried to love them unconditionally. I kept searching for lessons in the pain, convinced that the people who hurt me were my "teachers," so I continued to keep them in my life, even as they continued to hurt me.

I constantly hear similar stories from others who write to tell me they can relate to my experiences and asking for advice for how to deal with their own related issues. I receive messages and e-mails from my readers, viewers, and listeners who tell me they're also nonconfrontational because they believe it's unspiritual to be angry, or even just to hold their own and stand up for themselves. They judge themselves, convinced that it's their ego rearing its head.

In their quest to please others (believing that's the spiritual thing to do), many don't even stop to heal their own hurt or honor their own feelings. When the pain becomes unbearable, they spend hours pondering, "What is the lesson I'm missing?" or "What is it I need to learn from this?" Many have admitted to a deep-seated fear that if they get things wrong in life, they'll suffer dire consequences later, what's known as karmic retribution.

This is classic empath behavior. In our desire to be nonconfrontational and to get it right (to do things that cause the fewest ripples), we lose sight of the prize: our connection to our own inner mystic. This was the case for me. I'd lost that connection because it was buried under layers of the spiritual dogma that I'd taken at face value.

As empaths, we can put more faith in authority figures than in ourselves, even if they're self-proclaimed gurus—and even if the messages being espoused by such figures don't feel right to us. Even when everything inside us is saying, *No, no, no! This is not right for you!* a people-pleaser will *still* put more credence in what an authority figure has to say. Because we don't want to seem difficult, we can suppress or doubt our own inner voices, as I did. In the end, misguided or misconstrued spiritual messages can actually *erode* our trust in our inner guidance system, sending us spiraling downward into doormat-hood.

Being Spiritual Means Being Authentic

A true spiritual teacher, however, sees your greatness and teaches you how to see it in yourself. They show you by example how to trust your own guidance system, and thus help you awaken your own inner mystic and set yourself free from fear and dogma. Good teachers help you believe in *yourself* rather than cultivate a belief in *them*. Ultimately, they teach you to connect to the divinity that lies within you.

It took death for me to understand that one missing element in all my previous spiritual teachings was my own connection to this divinity within, or to God. Death taught me that I had to recognize my own divinity *first* before I could be or do anything of value to others. For the first time in my life, I realized that the divinity I sought outside myself was actually already within me. It was part of the life force we all have simply by being born. It's the gift of our birthright in being here, on this earth.

We are all spiritual. How can we not be? We come from Spirit and we return to Spirit. We don't need to "work at" being more spiritual. We need to realize that we are inherently spiritual beings and connect to the source of our own divinity, or our inner mystics. When we take time out to be quiet and still our minds, and do nothing but focus on our own breath, even for ten or fifteen minutes, it brings us back to our center. It's in that space where we do nothing but focus on our breath that our inner mystic, or the divine, can give us guidance.

Once I realized that I was an expression of the divine and had *shakti* (or *prana* or life force energy) running through me like everyone else, things started to fall into place. I started to get in touch with my inner guidance system again and cultivate my authentic spiritual self. I began taking more positive actions that circumvented my tendency as an empath to diminish myself. I trusted my intuition more instead of second-guessing the guidance I felt coming through. I stopped giving my power away to those who claimed to be in authority. Instead, I listened with my heart to see if I truly resonated with what they were saying, and wasn't afraid to ignore their guidance if it didn't resonate with me, or caused fear, or made me feel disempowered. I reminded myself that I'm connected to the same divine-force energy they are, so they didn't have the power to override what my intuition was telling me.

Performing these actions was the first step to integrating the power of self-love. I continue to do them. When I do, the right teachers, the right books, the right messages come to me at the right time. Every day, I read and hear stories about how this change in outlook and actions has opened the door for others to receive exactly what they need.

A common theme that seems to occur is when people need an answer to a personal dilemma or health-related issue, and they go to multiple channels to find their answers. They also research online, and in the end, they're even more confused, because they're receiving conflicting information. This is when I tell people to "Just stop. Quiet your mind and breath and turn inward. Visualize your connection to the divine, and know you are loved."

Those who've tried this practice have shared with me that they experience a level of peace and calm; and then subsequently, the answer comes to them. Even if it's from an external source—a book, a podcast, a colleague—it comes to them when they least expect it. One woman who'd been beating herself up for having a physical condition had spent all her time researching it. She shared with me that when she stopped and tried the practice of just becoming at peace with herself, she developed a deep love for herself she hadn't felt before. She continued to do the visualization and breathing practice, and on the fourth day, a friend dropped by with a book, saying, "I know you were researching this condition, and I came across this book and thought you might be interested." It turned out that book had all the information she needed to bring clarity to how to heal her condition! She'd never come across this book before, during all her research, and within weeks her symptoms reduced, and within months were gone completely.

Unconditional Love ≠ Doormat

At the same time, I hear from people all over the world telling me how hard it is to practice unconditional love, particularly toward people who are mean, abusive, or disrespectful toward them. They still feel resentment and anger, but struggle in their hearts to forgive. And that's because we're still taught that loving those who've hurt us—even if they're no longer an active part of our lives—is a spiritual virtue.

In fact, what we need to understand is that it's more important to love and value *ourselves* first. Without self-love we remain doormats no matter how much spiritual work we do. That's why I consider self-love a key element missing in most spiritual practices. When we love and value ourselves, we no longer feel the need to work at forgiving the perpetrator. But sometimes we have to flip familiar spiritual dogma on its head.

For example, if someone hurts you or tries to walk all over you, the first step is not to try to love them unconditionally if it doesn't *feel* right to do so. It isn't to blame yourself or force yourself to love the other unconditionally if it doesn't feel genuine, or to judge yourself as unspiritual if you can't do so. And the first step in *that* process is to acknowledge that you've been hurt and parent yourself as though you are parenting your own inner child. You need to take care of your emotional well-being first. This is challenging for doormats, since we fall into the trap of trying to appease people who've hurt us, or win them over, or make them love us—all while trying to love *them* unconditionally.

To love others unconditionally does not mean letting others walk all over you. You can love these people and still set firm boundaries. You won't be banned from Nirvana. You won't rack up bad karma by taking care of yourself. Doing what's best for you (especially if you aren't giving others what they want) can be terrifying at first, but it becomes so much easier with time. You just need to find a method that you can work with. Recently, I was in a business situation where I was feeling exploited, frustrated, and vulnerable with a company I was doing business with. This organization had signed a one-year contractual agreement with me for the rights to some of my work. The agreement had expired, but they continued to use my material, and to advertise that I was one of their content providers. When I'd talk with them about this, they'd lead me to believe that another agreement from them was on the way. It felt as though they were keeping me hanging, not wanting to let me go, while at the same time, not committing or paying for a new lease on my rights. By that point, I wasn't even sure I wanted to sign up with them again, if this was how they were going to treat me. I had so many other projects going on at the time, and several irons in the fire, and didn't feel that I needed their business. Still, this situation made me feel like the child who'd been bullied at school—this organization was extremely prominent, so I didn't want to do anything to spoil the relationship, yet I didn't want to feel exploited.

I spoke to friends who suggested a course of action that would involve conflict and a level of aggression that made me feel uncomfortable. Then one person made a suggestion that really resonated with me. She suggested I appoint someone, perhaps a member of my own staff, as my business manager, and have that person approach the company and tell them that as our agreement with them had expired, we were about to pitch my body of work to other organizations. The business manager was to reiterate that we were coming to them *first* before taking it to anyone else, because of our past working relationship, which was why we wanted to give them first refusal (this was *Wu Wei* the bag of cookies, to disarm them, showing them that there were no hard feelings, and we were giving them something). Her advice resonated with me and I followed it immediately, appointing someone from my own team. My new business manager was firm and gave them a deadline and said that if we didn't hear back by then, we would be pitching the work to others.

What ended up happening was quite amazing. I felt so empowered by this approach because there was no conflict, and no hard feelings involved, and then suddenly, in that state of empowerment, I started getting offers from other companies. I ended up taking one of the other offers, but the respect I now get from the organization I felt was exploiting me has increased manyfold—they continue to circle back to me to see if I'd like to work on projects with them, and have kept their doors open to me, even though I didn't go with them.

After telling this story during one of my workshops, audience members started sharing their own experiences of handling conflict-infused situations in a nonconfrontational way, and how it had worked for them when they did it from a place of power, as opposed to coming from a place of doormat-hood. Gina, an author for a small publishing house, shared about how she'd been feeling exploited by her publishers. They were consistently giving her low-ball offers, even though she had a very good track record of book sales. She didn't have an agent, and because she wasn't well known, she struggled with finding one who would take her on. Gina was hesitant to confront the head of the publishing company to ask for a bigger advance, so she decided to send her manuscript to several publishers to see if anyone was interested. Not only that, she also calculated how much more she could earn if she chose to self-publish her book.

Gina managed to get interest from another small publishing company, and their offer was greater than what her current company was giving her. Armed with that offer, as well as her own calculations of what she could potentially earn if she self-published, she shared her findings with the head of the publishing firm. Even though Gina approached him very amicably, she had every intention of walking away if he didn't up his offer to meet what she was able to get elsewhere. After he saw her figures, he increased his offer because he now saw a greater value in her work.

To climb out of the doormat personality, we must be sure not to get caught up trying to make excuses for the one exploiting or hurting us, or to bend over backward to win them over, or to force ourselves to forgive those who've hurt us when we're not ready to, with the mistaken notion that forgiveness is supremely spiritual. Many of us struggle with the word "forgive," especially if we've been hurt very badly. But in the spirit of *Wu Wei*, consider replacing the word "forgive" with the word "release." In other words, instead of *forgiving* people, you're *releasing* them. You're releasing them from your life so they no longer have a hold on you. Simply change the question from *How do I forgive them?* to *How do I release them?* And then consider yourself, love yourself, and value yourself, and know you have the power to change the dynamics of any situation.

The Key to Self-Love

One of the methods I use to increase self-love is to write my way through my feelings. It's very cathartic. In your journal, log your responses to these questions:

- Do I judge myself too harshly?
- Do I allow people to walk all over me, and exploit me?
- Do I go to the ends of the earth to please other people, even to my own detriment?
- Do I feel tired and drained often?
- Do I seek out people who have hurt me, trying to win their approval?
- Do I fear disappointment?
- Do I make time for others but not for myself?
- Do I feel guilty when I do something nice for myself?

If you answer yes to any of these questions, it means there's plenty of room to love yourself more. You can make a list of the things you'd do if you did love yourself—and be really honest. For example, would you spend more time caring for yourself—taking the time to exercise more, going for a walk, perhaps shopping for and cooking more healthy foods, or spending quiet time in nature? (You will probably have crossover from your list about what to do to charge your batteries.) Maybe you'd go back to school and get that degree, or attend a workshop you've always wanted to attend. Make a nice long list, and even though you may not do everything, you can commit to doing one thing on the list each day, as a sign of self-love.

Loving ourselves infuses us with strength—the strength to love others and lovingly walk *away* from those who don't nurture our lives. One of the mantras I've created that helps me stay in this positive space is this: *I will only engage with those who are loving and appreciative toward me.* This mantra keeps me focused on those who treat me in an affirming and supportive way, rather than me draining my energy trying to win over people who treat me like a doormat.

Of course, we all have to engage with people who don't treat us in a loving way, whether it's a bullying boss, a difficult child, or an intolerant colleague. We can't avoid this. However, when your batteries are charged and your light shines, you have much more energy to deal with these issues without diminishing yourself or giving up your power. You deal with people and situations from a place of strength, instead of victimhood.

I want to be clear: Spiritual teachers and communities are important. The ones I've explored in my life were well-meaning and their messages were positive for the world at large. Just keep in mind, a spiritual teacher's true role in your life is to help you strengthen your inner guidance system, rather than strengthen your trust in them. Nourish yourself from within, from your own wellspring of divinity.

Meditation for Expressing Your Divinity

I recite these words often. The more you practice this meditation, the more you'll start to truly feel the divine energy and love flowing through you. These words can be a constant source of strength, so I encourage you to repeat them often.

> *"I am a facet of the divine and always connected to it.*
> *I am powerful and have access to everything I need.*
> *I feel my energy expanding as I visualize it.*
> *I am a spiritual being and I am loved.*
> *Love is my birthright and not something I have to work for.*
> *I release all doubts and fears within me.*
> *I am worthy and deserving and express myself unapologetically."*

Chapter 6

WHEN THE BODY REBELS

MANTRA:
"My body is smart! I choose to listen to my body."

As you build your spiritual connection, hone your intuition, deepen your connection to the web of consciousness, and develop a healthy ego, it's important to be vigilant about taking care of yourself and nurturing your love for yourself. Because empaths are so giving (often pathologically so), we can drain ourselves of our life force energy. I've discussed the need to recharge our batteries, and the fuel for those batteries is our life force energy.

Our path to healing needs to take our empathic tendencies into consideration, tendencies such as depleting ourselves, absorbing fears and illness, and, because our barriers are down and the opinions of others can feel like our own, our high suggestibility. It's important for us to learn to protect ourselves from taking on other people's illness or other people's opinions about our illness. And if we're ill, we need to know how to actively participate in our own healing process. We also need to help loved ones who are ill do the same.

The same need for prevention applies to health-care practitioners. Judith Orloff observes that empaths are attracted (and suited) to fields like doctors, nurses, and healers because we love to help people. We're natural-born rescuers, caregivers, and healers, and have the ability to intuit what others feel, so we go out of our way to make them feel better, which makes us great health-care practitioners.[1]

There must be plenty of doctors and nurses who are empaths absorbing all the sensory input within those hospital walls on a daily basis—not to mention dealing with their own stress from working long hours with patients. As an empath, if you're a doctor, nurse, or other health-care practitioner, and you're dealing with troubled, fearful, or sick people all day long, then the necessity for tools to mitigate absorbing symptoms of those who are ill becomes even more critical. You'll need to practice some kind of self-care protocol, otherwise you won't understand why you're always so exhausted and constantly experiencing the symptoms of others.

So if we're in the healing profession or caring for loved ones, how can we protect our own health? How can we be a caring, compassionate relative, friend, or caregiver without wiping ourselves out in the process? How can we empathize with someone who's ill without getting sick ourselves? And how do we keep from absorbing their emotions about their illness?

In the work I do, I attract a lot of people who have cancer and other health conditions that trigger deep fear within them. I always want to go out of my way to help them. Since my trip to Costa Rica where the shaman pointed out to me that I was lifting others up at the expense of my own energy, I've learned to take care of myself by developing a series of visualizations I do before conducting workshops, seminars, and retreats. I consciously create an energetic field around me (see the meditation at the end of Chapter 3) that protects me when I'm around people who are suffering from pain and ill health. I also make sure my life force energy is on high (see the meditation at the end of this chapter). By taking these simple steps I no longer develop physical illness from being near others who are ailing. Also, I've found that when my life force energy is on high, it naturally helps lift others. They tend to laugh more, feel lighter, and have mentioned that their fear seems to dissipate.

Healing Fear with Love

As I've said, my deep-seated fear of cancer started with Soni's diagnosis and my feeling that if she was susceptible to the disease, then I was, too. Before I go further, I need to make it clear that while my story is about cancer, and that's my point of reference, you may be dealing with a different illness. Whatever condition you're dealing with—MS, lupus, cystic fibrosis, allergies, chronic infections—the ideas, concepts, and observations in this chapter still apply.

Soni was a strong and vibrant woman, the last person I thought would be vulnerable to disease. Yet she was. Then, within a few months of her diagnosis, we received news that my husband, Danny's, brother-in-law had also been diagnosed with an aggressive form of cancer. This news anchored the fear even deeper in me because both these people were close to my age. I began researching everything I could about cancer and its causes. Initially, I started doing this in the hope of helping; I wanted to be there for Soni, to help her fight. But I found that the more I read about the dis-ease, the more I was afraid of everything that could potentially cause it. I started to believe that everything created cancer—pesticides, microwaves, preservatives, genetically modified foods, sunshine, air pollution, plastic food containers, mobile phones . . . This obsession progressed until, eventually, I started to fear life itself.

Danny's brother-in-law and Soni were going through the full treatment: chemotherapy, radiation, surgery, stem cell—everything. And I didn't see them getting better. It increased my fear. I feared the treatment of cancer. And I feared death. I wanted to do everything I could to avoid cancer. Everything I did was driven from a place of not wanting the dis-ease. My research broadened to include how to avoid cancer. I purchased all the supplements that were antioxidants and anticancer—curcumin, CoQ_{10}, Omega-3, chlorella, vitamin C, green tea extract. I took boat-loads of these supplements every day. I grew my own wheatgrass so I could take fresh wheatgrass shots every morning, made super-green smoothies, and started to follow an anticancer diet—collard greens, kale, lentils, and lots of raw foods.

Others I've spoken with, no matter what dis-ease they're dealing with or are fearful of getting, have done the same, perhaps eating a raw plant-based diet, going as far as curtailing attendance to any social events; or if they do socialize, bringing their own food. Although it's good to eat healthy, the problem with anti-cancer diets or anti-dis-ease diets, or anti-anything is that the focus is on what you're against. An anti-cancer diet keeps your focus on the dis-ease, and not on health, and with the empath's high level of suggestibility, we're even more susceptible to the illness we're guarding against or trying to heal from. Today, my focus is on being healthy, active, vibrant, and joyful, and I do what it takes to maintain that state. I no longer focus on dis-ease. I believe in increasing wellness, rather than focusing on eradicating illness.

But back then I was obsessed. I changed my diet depending on the latest article I'd read, the newest findings. Danny and I installed a reverse-osmosis water system. We measured our electromagnetic field (EMF) readings to determine if we needed to make any drastic changes in our environment. I was determined that I wasn't going to get cancer because I was so vigilant and I was fighting against the illness. If I missed a dose of my gazillion supplements, I felt incredibly fearful, and would make up for it by being even more vigilant. I was exhausted from my self-prescribed protocol, working extremely hard every single day at keeping cancer away. My focus was completely on cancer. And you know what happened? I got cancer.

So here's the thing: I realized—and I didn't realize this from having cancer, but from dying from cancer—that the focus is not supposed to be on avoiding illness but on living life, on being passionate about life, immersing ourselves in living our lives fully.

I didn't realize this at the time, but the actual act of working super hard just to stay healthy sends our own psyche the message that our body doesn't have the capacity to stay healthy without intervention. Dr. Bruce Lipton, author of the bestselling book *The Biology of Belief*, discusses the "innate healing ability" we're born with, going on to say that "from the age of about six, our brain patterns alter. We start acquiring perceptions about who we are in the world, and in the majority of cases, our conditioning overrides this natural ability."[2] In my case, the conditioning was "Staying healthy requires hard work on my part." Others have told me that their conditioning was "We live in a toxic environment" or "I have a weak constitution" or "Illness is in my family" and other such self-sabotaging beliefs.

Another reason why empaths seem to be susceptible to illnesses is because of our tendency to take on the problems of everyone around us (and sometimes even the problems of the world), and make them our own. We feel it's our responsibility to help and fix everything, and it bothers us if we can't. In fact, we may even feel guilty if we can't fix these problems, and mitigate that guilt by suffering with others. In other words, "If you're suffering, and I can't help you, then I'll suffer with you."

One small-business owner wrote to me that she felt guilty if any of her staff were working late, so she'd stay until every last one of them left the office, even though all her work was done. She ended up going home late every single night even though most of her team of fifty averaged only one late night per month. That's how I was with Soni—the guilt, the suffering right along with her. In my case, my illness was my body's way of saying, "Enough is enough!" Sometimes this is the only way our bodies can get us to let up.

A quotation by Esther Hicks, who, along with the late Jerry Hicks, is the author of *Ask and It Is Given: Learning to Manifest Your Desires* and *The Law of Attraction,* put it very succinctly: "You cannot get sick enough to help sick people get better. You cannot get poor enough to help poor people thrive. It is only in your thriving that you have anything to offer anyone."[3] So empaths need to take special care to put ourselves first, to love ourselves as though our lives depend on it, because they do. Here's how.

4 Keys to Healing

Knowing what I know now, if I had to deal with a health crisis, I'd handle it very differently than I did the first time. Previously, the first thing I did was speak to doctors about treatment options. I also consulted Dr. Google (which is a sure way to terrorize yourself!) and checked all the options available to me, including alternative options, and everything else that was out there. Well-meaning friends, who also researched, inundated me with additional information—a lot of it contradictory—that led to confusion, fear, and even more stress. In addition, all this information was focused on healing at the physical level, which to me means managing the symptoms, focusing on the illness itself—the trajectory, statistics, probable outcomes—rather than on underlying causes and wellness. The steps I would take today if diagnosed with a serious illness, and what I suggest to you, are the opposite. I've listed them here, in order of importance.

1. Ask, "What can I say 'no' to?"

If you have a hard time saying "no" and a tendency to take on more than you can or should, the first thing to do is ask yourself, *Where am I taking on things that I don't want to do?* In other words, *Where can I say "no"? Where have I been saying "yes" when I meant "no"?*

You might be someone who has a tendency to rescue people or help them, even when they don't ask for it, or don't need it. Perhaps your fear of disappointing people perpetually drives you to take on much more than is necessary, and you eventually add layers and layers of issues that are not originally your own.

You can use this step for the most minor ailments. I do. If you feel a flu coming on, or aches and pains, make a list of all the things you're currently tackling but don't want to do, and one by one, pluck up the courage to say "no." You won't regret it.

Certainly there are times you don't really want to do something because it's draining or tiring, but you still have to do it—circumstances such as caring for the well-being of someone in need, like a special needs child or an aging parent. These responsibilities may involve people we love. If you have those situations, acknowledge them. Acknowledge that this takes up a lot of your energy, and then give yourself space to recover the energy by doing something that makes you happy. Recharge your battery.

It's very important that you don't judge yourself for needing to take care of yourself. Give yourself permission to be okay with taking time out without feeling guilty and do something you enjoy, something just for you, whatever that might be.

Also, there are ways you can turn responsibility into fun projects or games, especially if you're taking care of young children. Make your responsibilities and chores as fun and creative as you can. Sometimes lightening your burden is just a mindset more than anything else.

2. Learn to open your receiving channels.

It's important to discover where you're not allowing yourself to receive, and if you're too focused on pleasing others, or doing for others without receiving, focus on learning to receive more.

Start with small things. For example, if someone pays you a compliment, accept it with grace and say, "Thank you" instead of deflecting it. If someone gives you a gift, don't feel the pressure of having to figure out how to make it up to them. Allow that opportunity to come organically; otherwise the feeling of obligation spoils the gift.

For those who find it hard to receive and are unable to say "no," a health crisis can often be the body's way of rescuing us from our current path in life, or obliging us to change, much like what happened to me when I felt too guilty to do anything for myself when Soni was sick.

3. Get passionate and excited about life.

Next, find ways to get excited about life. Ask yourself, *If I had a clean bill of health right now, what would I do with the rest of my life?* And, whatever the answer, start to do it, or at least work toward doing it.

Chances are, the health challenge is a wake-up call, signaling that the way you're currently spending your life is depleting your life force energy. Most of us tend to focus on the illness, trying to figure out how to eradicate it, and then we go back to the life we were living prior to the illness, which is the life that brought us the illness in the first place. So it's important to connect with what fills you with excitement and joy.

Ask yourself, *Why do I want to get well? Why do I want my life back? Do I want to go back to a life that was depleting my energy? Would I spend more time with the people I love? Would I do more exciting things? Take more vacations? Work less? Do what makes me happy? Follow my passion? Discover what is truly my passion?* Those are the things I suggest exploring while you're going through the healing process, because the idea is to get passionate about living life, and to have a reason to live, a reason to be healthy and strong and want a long life.

To me, one of the biggest determining factors of my health is my reason for living. What is my reason for being? Do I feel I have a purpose? I want to be clear about the reasons why I live and the reasons why I stay healthy. There is no incentive to be healthy if you feel trapped in a life you hate.

If I were dealing with a health challenge, I would go on a road to self-discovery. If you have a burning desire to be or do something, don't suppress it, because that's your calling. I love the term "calling" because, to me, it feels like my future self is calling me forth into my future.

A clue to finding your calling is to use your *imagination*. When I set my imagination free, I connect with something that's exciting and beautiful: For me, it's my sixth sense, my intuition, and my higher self. When I describe this connection to people, usually their response is, "Oh, it's your imagination." But imagination is what has *unveiled* my calling and my purpose to me. It has helped me to connect with my spirit, my soul.

Many of us have somehow been conditioned to believe that if we follow our desire and we follow our calling, we're actually being selfish. No. What you're actually doing when you suppress your imagination, when you suppress your desires, when you suppress your calling, is suppressing that which you came here to be and do.

I have learned that my soul, my spirit, my higher self, uses my imagination to communicate with me. I believe this is true of all of us. As Albert Einstein wrote, "Imagination is more important than knowledge. For knowledge is limited, whereas imagination embraces the entire world, stimulating progress, giving birth to evolution."[4] So if you want to find your place in the universe, and your connection to the all-that-is, unleash your imagination.

4. Ask, "How can I support my body? What are my treatment choices?"

When we're struck with a health issue, the first thing we tend to look at are treatment options. Knowing what I know today, if I had a health issue, and it wasn't a medical emergency, I would put treatment options farther down on the list of importance. That's because jumping right into looking at treatments can create fear, and the priority is first taking care of yourself and *not* doing it from a place of fear. As Dr. Joe Dispenza says in the foreword of Kelly Noonan Gores's book *Heal*, stress "can knock our body out of balance."[5] We need to be in a state of rest to heal. So the first step is removing that fear and its stress on your body, and then reviewing treatments will be less stressful and more likely to work.

Therefore, I believe that the fourth priority is to learn how to support your body. Look at what your treatment choices are as you go through this journey of discovering your passion and purpose. You can still work at figuring out your treatment options, but I would keep your focus on steps 1, 2, and 3 as being of greater importance, even though in the traditional medical paradigm they're not even factored into treatment plans.

When looking at treatments to support your physical body, I suggest choosing options that make you feel safe and empowered. And choose to work with health-care practitioners who make you feel that way, too.

Here's an example of an interaction I had with my primary care doctor who refused to listen to my own knowledge of my body. I went to the doctor for a regular checkup. Everything in my checkup was fine with the exception of my blood pressure, which was high. I was surprised, because I usually have lower than normal blood pressure. So I asked her to retake it. Once again, it was high. The doctor was alarmed and told me to come back in a few days to check it again.

A few days later I returned. My blood pressure was extremely high. She prescribed medication to lower my blood pressure. I loathe taking medication, so I tried to argue, asking if there were any natural products that could do the job, but she was determined, and said, "No, I cannot count on natural products for this." I went on the blood pressure meds, and after a few days, I started feeling really strange—a bit weak and faint. So I went back to see the doctor, and my blood pressure was within the normal range. Considering I was taking the medication, there was nothing surprising there. Despite my side effects, the doctor insisted that I stay on the meds, because they were working.

After another week of feeling a bit weak and faint, I decided to buy my own blood pressure meter from the drugstore. Upon checking, I saw that my blood pressure was unusually low—well below the normal range.

So I skipped taking the medication for a couple of days and then took my blood pressure. It was normal. I kept checking during the next few days, and found it to be normal, without the meds. I couldn't figure out what was going on, except it only seemed to register high at the doctor's office. I Googled "high blood pressure at doctor's office" and saw that it was very, very normal for people's blood pressure to spike when they were being tested by a doctor. It's a condition called "White Coat Syndrome," meaning that our stress levels go up when we are seeing a doctor. When I went back to the doctor with my findings, she just shrugged it off. She was well aware of White Coat Syndrome. She did not suggest I continue the medication.

Feeling uncomforted by this doctor, I found another one who welcomed my input and honored exploring alternative treatments (in this case, natural) with me. This doesn't mean that doctors should invite us, as patients, to self-diagnose and prescribe, but that our opinions, instincts, and preferences should be considered.

You want to work with someone who understands you and understands how to work with empaths, and aligns with how you perceive the world. For example, empaths can be particularly sensitive to hospitals and feel fear easily, so choose a practitioner who doesn't instill fear of illness in you, and instead encourages you to focus on healing and creating a life of health and wellness. Whether you choose conventional treatments, alternative treatments, or a combination of both, check in with yourself to see whether these treatments make you feel as though you're on the road to wellness and health or if you feel they're damaging your body. It's important to choose what makes you feel like you're on the road to healing.

I suggest rejecting doctors or treatment options that make you feel extremely fearful of the dis-ease. Previously, I felt fear if I followed the suggested protocol, and fear if I rejected it. I gave complete power to my doctors because I didn't want to displease them, and I feared going against what they were telling me, even though my intuition was screaming that I needed something more. As a result, I doubted my own abilities, and the more I doubted myself, the sicker I got.

I've heard stories from participants in my workshops who have experienced similar things. One woman took matters into her own hands. She was feeling tremendous fear over her prognosis, and felt that her doctor wasn't helping by keeping her focused on the dis-ease, instead of on her journey to healing. So she plucked up the courage to "fire" her doctor, and find another one. She had to get her family on her side first, which she did successfully. She then consulted a doctor who came highly recommended by an empath friend of hers, and with this new doctor, she felt much more empowered, more in control of her journey to wellness. She went on to make a full recovery, but remarked on how much easier it was with a doctor who supported her in focusing on wellness, as opposed to focusing on going to battle with her own body while fighting the dis-ease. With her new doctor, she was able to stay much more positive and joyful through the journey, instead of being in a constant state of fear.

The body is much smarter, stronger, and more resilient than we've been led to believe. Our state of mind and emotions are key to the healing process; we need to take care of our emotional well-being first, trust the people who are treating us, and trust that they're also sensitive to our mental and emotional well-being.

When faced with different treatment options, whether conventional or alternative, such as energy healing, I would ask you to ask yourself, *Which of these treatment options makes me feel more empowered? If I were to imagine my life force energy, which of these options makes me feel like I'm increasing life force energy within me? Which options make me feel like I am nurturing myself?*

Go for what resonates with you and work with a team of people who support your choices. Your health caregivers need to make you feel good about your choices, not confuse you or make you feel fearful because your choice isn't the direction in which they would have gone. Try not to surround yourself with people who make you doubt your choice of treatment. You need to feel good about it, and they need to make you feel that you're on the road to wellness. You also want to be with health-care workers who are going to support your choices of how to get you from where you are now to health, and then on to thriving. You want to work with a team of people that can do that, and surround yourself with others—friends, family—who are also going to support your choices.

When I went through my illness, I was surrounded by people with different opinions about what I should do, and all those opinions added to my confusion. I would make sure that that doesn't happen next time. I would surround myself with people who are either on board with my choices and helping me and encouraging me, or I would stay away from them until I got my clean bill of health.

Optimizing Your Life Force Energy

I want to go a bit deeper into the concept of life force energy here. Again, life force energy is also known as *prana* or *shakti*—the power or cosmic energy that flows through each of us. To me, healing is all about optimizing our life force energy, drawing on that energy to allow the body to heal it, instead of relying on drugs, surgery, and other procedures. However, it's also important not to deny the need for these modalities when you do need them—sometimes your life force energy may be so depleted that you may need the help of drugs or surgery to buy you time, while you learn to optimize that energy for yourself.

To explain in more detail what I mean by "optimizing your life force energy," I ask you to use your imagination a bit. Earlier, I asked you to imagine that you could *see* your life force energy, and I asked you to imagine what it would look like. This exercise builds on that one.

So now, find a quiet place where you won't be disturbed, and, if possible, maybe play some soothing music.

The Healing Sanctuary

Imagine you're in a beautiful healing sanctuary, sitting in a comfortable reclining armchair. A technician straps a band to your wrist that measures your emotional and energetic responses. It's connected to a little screen that the technician can monitor.

She has a list of questions designed to elicit emotional responses that register on the device's screen. As the technician asks you each question, you'll notice that your emotions shift as you think about it, as well as when you think about your answer. You might feel joy when you think about your children, or your pet puppy, or a loved one. Perhaps your heart sinks when you think about someone who drains your energy or your job, if it's something you don't enjoy. As you experience these feelings, you'll notice on the meter that your energy levels register either above or below your original baseline, depending on what you're feeling. You can create your own mental scale, and rate how your energy feels with each question, perhaps rating your energy between 1 and 20.

Everything is being recorded on the device, as the technician goes through what seems like dozens of questions—and various permutations of those questions—depending on what you answer.

You can create your own list of questions; go with additional questions that might pop into your mind during the exercise. For now, these are the questions she asks. As you imagine her asking each question, take the time to register your response in your body and on the screen.

- Are you lonely?
- What are your current relationships like?
- Are there people in your life whom you love, and who love you?
- Do you feel that your life has purpose and meaning? If so, tell me about it.
- Do you feel that your life has joy?
- What sort of things bring you joy and make you happy?

- What makes you feel fearful? What causes stress?
- How do you feel about your current financial situation?
- Do you like what you spend your days doing? If not, do you feel you're doing what you do because you have to? That is, because you have no choice, or are trapped?
- When you think of your childhood, what or how do you feel? (Love? Warm and fuzzy? Drained and fearful?)
- When you think of your family, what do you feel? (Love? Warm and fuzzy? Drained and fearful?)
- Are there specific members of your family who make you experience these feelings? (Love? Warm and fuzzy? Drained and fearful?)
- Do you have pets? If so, what does it make you feel like to spend time with them, or think about them?
- Are there people in your life who drain you? Do you have to spend time with them?

After completing this set of questions, the technician asks you about the different foods you eat.

1. What are your favorite foods?
2. What are your least favorite foods?
3. What foods do you love to eat but don't because you think they're unhealthy?
4. What foods don't top your favorites list but you eat them because you believe they're good for you?
5. What foods do you love to eat that *are* good for you?
6. What foods do you love to eat—and do eat—that *aren't* good for you?

One by one, she asks you to think of these foods, and then she checks to see how they register energetically on the meter—which foods increase your energy and which decrease your energy? In many cases, the answers may surprise you.

For example, ice cream may actually increase your energy because of the joy it brings you when you eat it, whereas wheatgrass juice may be decreasing your energy because you hate the way it tastes. All this time, you may have been avoiding ice cream, believing it to be bad for you, while drinking wheatgrass shots, believing them to be healthy. It's also possible that your energy may register high on products like wheatgrass juice because you feel you're doing something good for your body, and that satisfaction in and of itself may cause you to register high energy levels.

Next, the technician asks you to think about different activities. Your energy level is measured against the type of exercise suggested, to see which ones make you feel more joyful, triggering higher levels of life force energy to be released. You can create this list beforehand or as you go. Here are some examples.

1. What types of exercise do you like best? If the answer is yoga, you can break it down into types of yoga—hot yoga, kundalini, hatha, *vinyasa*. If it's swimming, do you prefer a pool, a lake, or the ocean?

2. What types of nights out do you most enjoy? If it's dining out, what type of food do you prefer? What type of restaurant— casual, formal, a picnic? Maybe it's going to the movies. If so, what genres bring you the most joy?

3. Music: This is one of my favorites. Different genres of music elicit different states of mind and different levels of energy. You're given the opportunity to listen to a range of music, and your energy levels are measured and recorded. Because the response to music is subjective in part, you'll know exactly what

music increases your energy. This exercise would allow you to tailor the music you listen to so that you can optimize your energy levels and increase healing.

4. Everyday activities. Do you like going to the mall, grocery shopping, driving, spending time with loved ones over dinner?

5. Vacations. Maybe you prefer a bike trip, camping, a guided tour, hiking or climbing, or visiting major metropolitan areas, remote villages, or sacred sites. Maybe a Baltic cruise does it for you, or relaxing for days on end at a luxury resort.

Evaluation

After answering these questions, you'll receive a full evaluation of your results (for the sake of this exercise, you can review your answers to determine your results), which will provide you with information on these points:

- The key areas of your life that are currently depleting your life force energy, whether it's because you are lonely, or dislike your job, or whatever else comes to mind.
- What uplifts your energy. For me this might be watching comedies, listening to dance music, shopping for shoes, surrounding myself with people who make me laugh or those with whom I can be completely authentic.
- Who in your life drains your energy.
- How to uplift your energy (and charge your batteries), including how to do it very rapidly—for example, by tuning in to the right types of entertainment, or music, or plugging in to the right activities, or connecting with the right people.
- What types of foods uplift and fuel you and what types don't?

All this information is tailored for you personally, in line with the life you live. To help you keep your energy high (doing less of what depletes your life force energy and more of what adds to it), in the healing sanctuary I envision, a personal counselor, or coach, will help you through issues such as self-love, worthiness, your life purpose, and dealing with loneliness. They'll also encourage you to listen to music, read books that feed your interests, and join classes like yoga or meditation, all of which would be available right there at the healing sanctuary. You will probably also be encouraged to take a break from technology, social media, and the news (at least for certain periods of time). And if you prefer to surround yourself with silence, there will be a place for that, too.

The idea is that if your life force energy is at a high level for a prolonged period, your body has its own capacity to heal, and it would direct that surplus energy toward healing. Chances are that if you're someone who's life force energy is very high and strong, your body would be physically healthy. And if not, I want to stress again a few of the common ways we deplete our life force energy, which may either lead to an illness or prevent our bodies from healing from one:

- We give of ourselves until we're drained, but we don't know how to receive.
- We don't know how to recharge our batteries.
- We feel guilty when we feel happy or do something good for ourselves.
- We don't believe we're worthy or deserving of positive things.
- We're stressed out all the time, perhaps by our relationships, our finances, or our jobs.
- We're lonely or grieving or suffering a trauma of some kind that goes on for a prolonged period of time.

If you're an empath who has a tendency to be a people-pleaser, have trouble saying no, take on duties and responsibilities you'd rather not, chances are you're depleting your energy, and with this device, you could instantly see when you're doing so.

Imagine that this device was a reality. We'd be able to clearly understand that if we're in these types of situations for prolonged periods of time, our bodies and our health will fail us. We would have a tangible result to show our coach or counselor, who would coach us out of these situations and help us create better coping skills and boundaries, and stronger self-esteem. Also, our coach (in this exercise, *you*) would help us build more situations that increase our energies. It's my dream that these healing centers will be a part of our future, but for now, you can play the role of patient, technician, and coach as you create your own therapeutic environment and learn more about your own life force energy. You can also take the role of the technician with someone you're helping, and ask that person the questions. Or, you might have someone else take that role with you.

One of the basic tenets of maintaining your life force energy is to surround yourself with those who will support your journey, and those who cause your life force energy to surge. I invite you to surround yourself with people who treat you as a normal person with dreams and aspirations, and not as "someone with" a chronic dis-ease. Surround yourself with those who speak with you as someone who is whole and has a bright future to look forward to. By surrounding yourself with people who uplift you, the dis-ease and the associated fear can be removed from your consciousness.

As Dr. Bruce Lipton, whom I mentioned earlier, writes in his book *The Biology of Belief*, "Thoughts, the mind's energy, directly influence how the physical brain controls the body's physiology."[6]

To me, this is a very powerful statement, coming from a cellular biologist, and it's echoed by Dr. Joe Dispenza in his book *You Are the Placebo*, where he discusses how thoughts drive physiological change. When you think new positive thoughts, they become feelings, which in turn "reinforce these thoughts." So, if you're not feeling well, "you need to think greater than how you feel . . . until it becomes a new state of being."[7]

Earlier, I mentioned that we're all part of a giant web, connected by an invisible "string"—and that this string is actually energy. Well, those of us with strong energy are sharing our energy with those whose energy is weaker, and this is a good thing. Knowing this, it's easy to understand that we have an obligation to do what it takes to make ourselves healthy and happy, so that we bring a happy, healthy self into the web, the world, and to our own families. That way, we will be contributing to the web of energy, instead of drawing from it.

Meditation to Increase Life Force Energy

You can do this meditation whenever you're feeling depleted or your spirits are low, or when you're feeling great and want to stay that way.

*"I visualize a beam of light coming down from above and entering
my body through my crown.
I allow the light to take on any color that it chooses.
As the beam of light enters my body, it bathes the inside of my head
and neck as it flows down into my chest.
It swirls all around the inside of my body, flowing down my arms
and legs, as it washes away all the tension in my body.
The beam of light is so powerful that it creates an aura around my
body.
I can control how bright I allow the light to glow; the brighter I
allow it to shine, the greater my aura.
The greater my aura, the more powerful my energy!"*

PART III

Your Relationship with
the World

Chapter 7

DYING TO BE *YOU*!

MANTRA:
"I am more than my physical body! I am an eternal being!"

From what I've experienced, read about, and learned from others, there are two stages of transformation in an empath's journey. I've discussed the first stage already; I encouraged you to recognize the traits of being an empath and offered ways for you to become aware of yourself. I experienced this stage during my NDE, though you might reach it through meditation, plant medicine, spiritual teachings, or an "aha!" moment while walking down the street—anything that causes you to experience the other realm, see heaven, or gain an expanded version of reality. It may also be clarity about why you're here on this planet.

The second stage, which could be seen as external, is about how you relate to the world after these transformational experiences. This stage is about integrating what we've experienced into our daily lives, and it's the one people struggle with more—for good reason. It's intimidating to maintain that sense of self-love and your connection to your inner mystic and the cosmic web of consciousness when car horns are blaring, or your phone's beeping with the sense of urgency and disconnect that can occur. So I want to let you know how to incorporate that inner awareness into the outside world.

What's in Your Marinade?

I refer to our own individual environment as our "marinade," the dominant culture in which we were indoctrinated, where there's a belief system we've adopted as our truth. We've all been marinated in a specific bath of thinking, believing, and behaving. A transformative experience temporarily lifts you from that marinade, and gives you a divine overview of life and your place in it. After such an experience, you don't quite fit into that dish of marinade anymore. Although each of us grew up in a different marinade, it's likely that the dominant belief system in yours is that we're separate individual beings—purely physical—and we have to compete with one another because there isn't enough (money, jobs, food, attention, praise, love . . .) to go around. In actuality, as I've said, we're all connected. But not everyone would agree.

When I first came back from my near-death experience, I was filled with the realization that everything I'd been taught to believe in ran counter to what I'd learned from the other side, which filled me with immense joy. I thought people would be interested to know what I'd learned. But when I started sharing, most people challenged me because everything I said was the opposite of what we're taught in schools, or by our culture, or by the current medical paradigm. Everything I learned ran counter to the dominant belief system on this planet, so it was really hard for people to believe what I was saying. I had to withstand naysayers and critics while holding on to what I'd learned. To withstand them, I used the keys I offer in this book—focusing on self-love, connecting with my inner mystic, listening to my intuition, and keeping my life force energy on high. I had to be myself fearlessly.

Even if we're armed with the knowledge that we can't be harmed no matter what happens in this reality—our energy never dies—it can still be very tiring and draining navigating this world when everyone around us has been conditioned to be suspicious of and hostile to anyone who's different or has a different set of values. It can also be extremely lonely. But you'll find your way. When you live from that authentic place, you'll soon attract others who see the world as you do, and you'll have more love and understanding for those who don't.

This is the dichotomy: If we have a transcendent experience and then try to live in this world and integrate our earthly experience with our transformative one, it can be challenging because others don't quite perceive reality the way we do. But if we have a profound, transcendent experience that causes us to escape the world and become a recluse, then there's no point in being here. We may as well stay in our realm of origin, the realm from which we come and to which we return after death.

So, again, and it bears repeating, the bigger challenge isn't in having a spiritually transcendent experience, but in integrating that experience into our earthly life once we "return." Once we've had such an experience, we can't forget it. It is nothing like a dream that comes during sleep and then dissipates with the dawning day—not at all. A spiritually transcendent experience feels more real than our earthly reality. Compared with the transcendent reality, the earthly one seems like an illusion . . . a dream. Forgetting this isn't an option. We can't unknow what we know. In fact, the more time that passes, the more real the experience feels, because we see all that we experienced in the transcendent realm panning out in our earthly life. Still, there will be times when we can lose sight of the experience because the physical reality can be incredibly persistent in making us doubt it, to believe only what we can perceive with our five senses, and so we need to create resources to be able to stay connected to that realm.

Many of my fellow near-death-experiencer friends I've connected with since my own experience would agree. Again, though, remember: This is the route *I* took to wake up, and a community I connect with, but there are many ways transformation can occur. One doctor I know gave up his medical practice after his NDE, which followed a near-fatal heart attack. After he regained his health, he became more involved in energy healing, because he now understood how important it was to feel higher states of energy for greater health. At first, his family wasn't happy with his decision because they were financially dependent on the income from his practice. However, for him, money was no longer a priority. He had clarity of purpose, and that overrode everything. Over time, his family learned to become supportive of his choice, because he knew this was his purpose, and he couldn't turn back.

A transcendent experience—however you arrive at it—is more like a portal that opens, inviting you to walk through it. It never really fades, and I think everyone that I've spoken to who has had an NDE or an awakening would agree on this. It's like a doorway that, once opened, never closes—so the clarity, or wisdom, never really disappears. Once you walk through it, your life is never the same as the one you left behind.

After coming back through that portal, my life was no longer what it had previously been. A new life opened up for me. In the weeks following my near-death experience, I watched my body heal beyond any medical doctor's expectations. Yet because I was in a state of invincibility, that healing felt normal to me. I understood now that I had always taken the victim role, but that, had I known to do so, I could have stepped into my own power at any time and become the creator of my own life. I learned that to be powerful I didn't have to wait for others to give me their approval. That power had always been there for me. I just couldn't see it because of the marinade I'd been soaking in. My marinade, or cultural conditioning, was one of victimhood, gender disparity, and believing I was inferior. All those beliefs and feelings were now gone. I could never go back to being the person I used to be—because the old me no longer existed.

So the bottom line is being true to the new you. Be yourself fearlessly. Everything else will fall into place.

Filters and Mirrors

Traumatic experiences make a deep impression on us; they lead us to take on lenses, or filters, through which we view the world, and through which we shape our lives. Your filters might be, *I live in a world where I have to work really hard to succeed because I have to compete with everyone to prove myself.* Or, *There's not enough to go around, and if I don't compete with people, they'll get it before I do.* Or, *I constantly have to prove my worth every hour of every day.*

Imagine if you'd been bullied as a child, or even been a victim of abuse. Or perhaps your parents held back approval. Any of these things can create damaging filters through which you view the world. These filters may cause you to be fearful of others, or untrusting of most people except for a very few. Maybe because of experiences in your life, you're suspicious of people you don't know. In other words, you view the world through a veil of mistrust. Or you're fearful, always expecting the worse outcome, and because of this, you're constantly playing it safe. Maybe, as we've discussed, you make choices based on the approval of others or you make your choices depending on which options involve less conflict.

Growing up, my physical differences and the subsequent teasing and bullying shaped me into believing that my physical appearance was inferior. One boy at school actually told me I was ugly. That stuck with me, and I believed it. Because I really bought into the beliefs that I was ugly and inferior, those beliefs became the lenses through which I viewed the world. As a result, I became extremely shy. I wanted to hide from the world, afraid of being seen because I didn't want people to judge me. My worldview made me an introvert. It made me small, and it changed who I thought I was. It affected my experience of everything around me.

But what if I'd been a child whose appearance was considered really beautiful or cute? The lens through which I viewed the world would be quite different from the one I had for years, and I would have had a completely different experience of the world.

Of course, that lens of being beautiful and fabulous can bring about its own problems later in life—perhaps if you lost your looks, it might bring about an insecurity you never experienced before—but for the most part, our childhood experiences seem to shape how we view our world to a large and seemingly permanent extent.

Although we can't control what happened to us in childhood, as adults we still seem to carry that baggage with us, often without realizing it. We still view the world through that same old lens that no longer applies! We may think we're seeing the truth, but actually we're viewing the world through our own filters. For example, as an adult I was boarding a flight and was singled out for a random security check. I immediately thought, *I'm being profiled because of my race.* Now, it may truly have been a random security check, but my head assumed it was racial profiling because I'd been racially discriminated against while growing up, and that created a lens through which I viewed my reality.

I had no idea how affected I was by my filters until I was at a social gathering and bumped into a guy I'd known when we were both nineteen. I'd had a crush on him way back then, but thought I wasn't pretty enough for him. But here's a surprise: As we were catching up, he let on that he'd actually liked *me* a lot, and had wanted to get to know me better and go out with me, but that I always seemed distant.

I was shocked to hear that I had seemed distant. That was quite a revelation for me. He then went on to say, "One of the things I found most appealing about you was that you had *no idea* how attractive you were."

That conversation showed me how we can still continue to view the world through these filters we created as children, and our negative feelings about ourselves can become self-fulfilling prophecies, causing feelings of rejection. In my case, I ended up perpetuating my own belief that

I wasn't worthy. This is how we create our reality and our world around us, based on our past conditioning.

We've been conditioned to believe that our perception of external reality is *the real world,* and that our internal conditions are merely responding to what's happening on the outside; whereas in actuality, *it's the other way around.* Since our perception of reality is skewed by our filters, we're reacting to a skewed reality, without even realizing that our external reality is mirroring our inner self.

We must be able to see past these filters so that we don't buy into what others are telling us to believe about reality. And we don't slide back in a need to conform and be accepted. We can do this by using the tenets I've taught in this book—loving ourselves, consulting with and listening to our inner mystic, and connecting with the cosmic consciousness. We get bigger instead of getting smaller to fit a false notion of who we are.

Navigating Without Filters

When I had my near-death experience, it felt as though all the filters just dissolved, and I saw myself for who I truly am. I realized I wasn't my body, my image, my race, my culture, my gender, or anything else I felt set me apart. These were all filters that are part of this physical realm, opinions we form about our gender and race, and so on, that become the filters through which we judge or evaluate others.

The dominant belief system here is that we are physical beings and nothing more, and the outer reality is the real world. That our inner world is purely our imagination. If we don't like our outside world, it is believed, we can change it by hard work, manipulation, coercion, or brute force. All these methods are attempts to exert some form of external control.

My near-death experience and the transformational clarity of so many I've read about and heard from; ancient wisdom teachings; and the quantum physics findings cited earlier all indicate that the truth is the opposite of our dominant paradigm on this planet. If we don't like the condition of our lives, we have to look at our inner world, and perhaps work on loving ourselves more. We have to look at dropping our filters and beliefs, so that our inner world can shine through and be reflected onto the outer, physical world.

Life after transformation can be even more challenging for empaths, people-pleasers, and those who have allowed themselves to become doormats. As I've said, empaths straddle two worlds—the physical (outer) one, and the personal (inner) one. Because empaths are so sensitive to our inner world, we constantly experience insights and guidance leading to transformational thoughts. However, because transformation comes from inside, even the most powerful transformation can be challenging to integrate when you're a people-pleaser. That's because you're so conscious of what others are thinking and desiring from you, and you want to fit in and not displease anyone.

Many of our filters are fear-based, causing us to believe we're not good enough. Imagine taking off your glasses and seeing the world differently! What would the world, the people in it, your view of yourself, look like if you removed the blurry filters you've accumulated over a lifetime? Without these filters, you could see not only how you have been operating through them, but also, how others are operating through their filters, such as those of fear, scarcity, or inferiority.

In my second book, *What If This Is Heaven?*, I spoke about buying into beliefs that don't serve us. That's really what filters are. We then navigate the world through these beliefs, and they often can create a hellish life for us. Literally, when we remove these filters, life could actually be heaven. Heaven is actually here, because that connection to our infinite, magnificent self is available to us all the time.

So how do we drop our filters? That's what I'd like to talk about, because if we become aware of them and drop them, it becomes easier to get in touch and stay in touch with our own true selves. One of the first things to ask yourself is, *What are my filters? What are the filters through which I perceive life?* In my case, since I was bullied as a child and racially discriminated against, I became a doormat and made myself a people-pleaser. The filter through which I perceived life was: *I am a victim of my circumstances.* At this point in my life, while these old thought patterns and attitudes come up, I'm aware of the part they played in how I perceived the world and lived my life, and because I'm aware, they generally have no hold on me. And with that awareness, I can imagine seeing without them, which takes me one step closer to removing them.

Let me give you a tangible example of how to detect your filters and remove them. I've had people tell me that they feel themselves slipping back into their old filters and belief systems. For example, they may have a creative idea for the direction in which they want to take their work that they can feel in their gut will be a success, and then their old filters of fear or doubts slip in. They start to feel, *This has probably been done before. I'm sure I'm not the only one with this idea. This can't be anything new.*

Claudia, an amazing singer, told me about an audition she went on. She was excited, keyed up, nervous, ready to knock it out of the park—feeling all these emotions at once. But then, just before her turn, she felt her throat tighten, and then the thoughts sneaked up on her: *Who do you think you are, believing that you can be a professional singer? This is just a childish dream!* She was furious with herself. *This is not the time,* she told the voices. *Visit later if you have to, but not now.* The more she tried to push the voices away, the more persistent they became.

When you feel these feelings—heaviness, sadness, anger, a tightness in your throat or shortness of breath, or you feel yourself freezing, that means your old filters are starting to slip back in. This is the signal to pull back and consciously dissolve them. One way of doing it is to visualize the filters around you actually dissolving and setting you free to follow your dreams!

Claudia made it through the audition, though she didn't get the part. She was determined, though, and the next time, she took a deep breath, and pictured those filters dissolving, and imagined seeing without them. It worked, and she started getting more and more jobs.

A few years ago, I was a featured speaker at a multispeaker event. After hearing one of the other speakers give his talk, which I thought was great, I went up to him in the speakers' lounge and told him I'd loved his speech. His response seemed a bit distant, and my filter interpreted his reaction as being cold, standoffish, and possibly borderline condescending. In other words, my victimhood filter was telling me that he felt superior to me and I wasn't good enough to be taking up his time chatting with him.

I'm so glad that later in the day I had the clarity of mind to realize that it was my filter kicking in. This is what I mean about being aware of our filters. When we're aware, we can more quickly spot when they're affecting our vision. Don't hesitate to question them, especially if they're patterns that come up time and again. The minute I said to myself, *It might have been my filter that was interpreting that exchange,* I started to receive a divine "download," or "voices," as I call them, and they said something like this: *That person is actually a big fan of your work and was taken by surprise when you went up to him! He's actually in awe of you and didn't know what to say!*

For me, these downloads come to me in what I refer to as "voices" from guides, or higher self, or inner mystic tapping into the cosmic toolbox of knowledge. They're not actually voices. An entire dialogue can happen in an instant—like a snapshot of words, and then I just know. It may not be the same for everyone. For others, it may be impressions, visuals, a sense of knowing, a ringing in the ears, a feeling like an electrical current, or a mixture of different things. Usually, you'll know what it means and what it's trying to tell you.

To say that I was surprised by that message is an understatement. *Whoa,* I thought. *You're kidding me! There's no way that someone would be in awe of me! I mean, I'm the small doormat person.* That's what my head was saying, or, more precisely, what my filter was saying, while there was another download being simulcast into my mind.

This other voice can only communicate with you if you can silence the thoughts the filters kick up, or at least question them, even for a brief moment. Filters can only influence you if you agree with them; negative filters only have power over you if you accept their judgments. But you don't need to accept them. That's the power you have. Question them whenever they poke their scruffy heads into your awareness. Always.

If you hold onto your negative filters too tightly, that higher "voice," "download," or what have you can't get through. It's as though the voice is on another frequency from that of the filter. You have to rise above your filter to the frequency of the guiding voice. And that voice will surprise you because it will say things *about* you and *to* you that you would never imagine for yourself; it would never occur to you to think those things. Note that the voice above your own filter is always encouraging, not discouraging. It's always inspiring, not fearful. It always takes you closer to an awareness of your own divinity.

I went back to look for that other speaker later, with this new feeling and renewed energy, Sure enough, I found out that he'd read my books and followed my work, and was a huge fan! He had felt awkward and shy when I'd gone up to him earlier because he had no idea I'd been in the audience watching him. He said he was so happy to finally be speaking with me in person. I was so glad I'd listened to my inner voice, trusted it, and taken the chance to go back to look for him. Otherwise, I would have missed the opportunity to get to know another wonderful person who has enriched my life. So you want to constantly check in and listen, because your life without these filters can open up opportunities and ways of seeing that you never would have imagined.

Tuning In

To develop a stronger connection to your infinite self and our spiritual guidance system, I'd like to first invite you to your filters—the filters that prevent you from reaching the frequency at which divine downloads occur.

People often ask me, "Why is it that *you* feel guided and others don't? Why are you special?" My response is that I'm not. I'm neither special nor chosen. These downloads—or, for me, voices—are communicating with us all the time, but it's up to us to tune in to their frequency so we can hear, see, or feel them.

Imagine what your life would look like if the lenses just came off and you didn't have those filters. Once you feel the lenses falling off, listen for the voices—the positive thoughts, ideas, insights, and hunches that come to you as you listen. If you have trouble hearing, seeing, or otherwise sensing and receiving downloads, start taking more time alone. In fact, spend more time talking to yourself. I know people say talking to yourself is the first sign of madness, but I promise you, if I'm mad, I'd rather be me than a lot of people out there who are considered sane. From what I've seen, most of the people in the world aren't that happy, whereas I truly feel happy. And it's not a fake, on-the-surface positivity thing. It's a deep-down happy, where, even if I'm going through a rough day, in my core, I still feel happy and secure. I no longer even feel the need to *think* about being happy, or to *act* happy or positive. I just *am* happy.

So what do I mean by talking to yourself? You can ask yourself questions, perhaps just before you go to bed, questions like, *What are my filters? Filters, please show yourself to me!* You will find that filters can be most often identified by the negative thoughts they tell you about yourself. They are the voices that keep us from loving ourselves and others. Or if you've identified your filters, you can ask, *How do I let go of my filters? Please help me, infinite self! Show me how to do this!*

You may get some answers in the middle of the night, or when you wake up in the morning. Keep a notebook and pen by your bedside, in case you're awakened with answers to your questions. You might want to write down both the questions you ask your inner self and the insights and answers that are revealed to you.

At first, the communication will feel subtle. You might doubt it, and think it's your mind. The way to differentiate your higher self from your mind is that your higher self will always give you something that feels really good, something you might not expect, some bit of wisdom, insight, or knowledge that feeds your soul, and showers you with love of self. Your past conditioning may try to bring in doubtful thoughts, and cause you to question the good thoughts you're receiving. For example, if you're about to try something new or something that's a stretch for you and you're feeling anxious, your higher self may give you a message such as "Don't fear this." Or if you've eaten something that has made you feel ill, you may receive guidance—as I often do—such as "Drink warm water." Your mind might try to dismiss these insights by countering with "Why would I be singled out to get messages like this?" or "It's just my imagination." You want to listen to the messages that make you feel as though you're cared for, protected, and loved, rather than those that are fear-based and make you feel worse, that cause you to doubt the love-based messages, the feeling of being loved and cared for.

That's how you differentiate between your higher self and your mind, or your lower, physical self. The voice of your lower or physical self is the one that usually comes from fear. It comes from anger. It comes from being a victim. It comes from the filters of your childhood that have built up over your life. The higher-self voice is the one that transcends all that. It's like the voice of the Divine or the voice of your guardian angels. It's the voice of someone who's extremely caring, the voice of unconditional love. So if you committed to entertaining only the thoughts that feel good, the ones that feed your soul, before the fearful thoughts and doubts set in to crash the party, that would be a good place to start.

The second thing to do would be to at least *act as if* those thoughts were true, and coming from your guides or higher self. Once you start trying them on, you'll notice how much better you feel about yourself, and about life itself. Soon, you'll see life start to mirror what you're feeling, and you'll keep going back for more. Over time, it will become easier and easier to listen and trust. The more you trust the messages coming through your higher self, the more such guidance you'll receive. The clarity of what's being communicated will begin to become stronger, too.

My higher self communicates with me continuously. It's continually guiding me about what to do next, what to turn down, and what to say yes to. It provides guidance on topics for videos, books, speeches, workshops, and retreats that helps me balance between the physical world and my connection with the nonphysical world. This guidance feels like a whole series of "aha!" moments. My inner voice is guiding me now, as I write these words, so much so that I feel as though I'm channeling. In fact, expressing this guidance in any form *is* a type of channeling. I just don't call it that, because calling myself a "channel" may attract people who want me to channel answers for them, and I want to encourage them to do that for themselves. My point is that *you* have access to *your* guidance the same way *I* have access to *mine*, and it's always more empowering to tune in to your own channel, by finding your own frequency, than tuning in to someone else's channel.

Here are some other ways to differentiate between the voice of your higher, infinite self, and the voice of your fear-based mind: Following your higher voice feels very light, and recharges your batteries, whereas following your fear-based mind drains you. Your higher self is unconditionally loving; your higher self will also never lead you to deliberately hurt or cause harm to other people, while your fear-based mind makes you feel less than as well as inadequate.

When you start to get into a flow where you're following your inner guidance, your life is working smoothly, and things are happening effortlessly, it will feel great. That's how I feel most of the time. However, there are times when I feel like something just knocks me out of my flow, as though I've been knocked out of my frequency. When I say knocked out of my frequency, I mean something occurs that knocks me back down onto a lower physical frequency, one where I can't hear my voices. For me, criticism does it, especially harsh criticism, meanness, or someone being nasty to me online. For others, the feelings and behaviors that can knock them out of that higher frequency are guilt, fear, anger, criticism, and seeking approval.

Be aware of when you feel as though you've been knocked out of your frequency and what causes it. When I speak about getting knocked into a lower frequency, I'm not saying that I'm on a higher frequency than others—not at all. I'm saying that the voice of our inner self is on a higher frequency than the voice of our mind, because our mind takes its cues from the outside world. It takes its cues from the environment and the paradigm in which we live, so the lower frequency means we're giving our power to those outside of us.

Here's how to raise your frequency: If something makes you feel down or dejected, or you're feeling that way and aren't sure why, think of a thought, feeling, or scenario a notch or two higher, and see how you feel a bit lifted. Look for joy in the things around you. Feel gratitude. Tune in. All these can help you lift your frequency. The more you listen to your inner mystic and feel the thoughts and insights that come to you resonate within your body, the more that will become your voice of authority. It makes you hum.

To raise your frequency, you might also visualize your aura expanding and getting bigger—that's what I do. I visualize my aura getting bigger and brighter, until I'm feeling like a ball of light, bright and powerful! Or you might picture one of the happiest times of your life, and think of your emotions during that time. Or think of someone you love, and how you feel about them—it could be your significant other, your child, or even your pet! All of these things are sure to shift your emotions and increase your frequency.

As an empath and people-pleaser, if you're the only one in your world who's removed your filters, you may find it hard to be different in a reality that's run by people who all have their filters on. You may find it more difficult to fit into a system that's created through everyone else's filters than others who are trying to integrate a transformational experience. You may find yourself being convinced by those around you that *you* are the one who's wrong or delusional, because *you* are the one who's different. After all, how could they *all* be wrong? *This* is the kind of thinking that can knock me out of my frequency. As empaths, that's one of the ways we get drained and sick; it's because we're trying to accommodate this dominant paradigm, while our inner truth is calling us, reminding us of what we really know and who we truly are.

When I get knocked out of my frequency, I know that my inner voice is still there, but my tuning needle has moved away from it. I just have to tune in to it again. If I spend my time defending myself with the critics or arguing with them, I end up draining myself because I'm spending more time at a frequency that's not my natural state. So I make sure not to respond or get involved, and even though I may lick my wounds for a little while and nurture myself, my focus is on getting back in touch with my inner voice.

When I do, that criticism acts as fuel for me to ask the questions that take me to another level of incoming messages from my guidance system. So I see this criticism as an opportunity to go deeper and raise my frequency. For example, it was through being painfully hurt by criticism that I understood how hard it is for empaths to share their messages fearlessly. In fact, this whole book, the themes within it, and the title *Sensitive Is the New Strong* are inspired by the pain I've felt when I encounter online trolls and critics. That pain prompted me to ask all kinds of questions:

- Surely, I'm not the only one who feels this much pain from criticism?
- Does this mean that all sensitive people are afraid of standing up and sharing their true life stories and extraordinary experiences?
- More important, are all sensitive people afraid of taking on leadership roles, or roles in the public eye, because they become targets for critics? Is this why there are so few empathic and sensitive leaders in our world?

- What if those of us who are empathic and want to change the world for the better could learn to be less afraid of criticism? Then, by stepping into the public eye, we'd be helping to pave the way for a new paradigm (instead of hiding behind the shadows of the bullies and narcissists).

Armed with these insights, I decided to keep moving forward, sharing my thoughts and feelings with the world, and my message that sensitivity and empathy may be our saviors if we want our species to survive. You see, if it wasn't for my own pain from the critics, I wouldn't have the fuel or the awareness to pave the way for other empaths and sensitive people to come forward and be seen, and take on leadership roles.

If I hadn't listened to my higher self, and only listened to my fear-based mind, I wouldn't be where I am today, doing what I do. If I'd listened to the critics, I would have stopped sharing my story and helping people a long time ago. I could have stayed on the frequency of doormat-hood and victimhood, but I knew that path had led me to getting cancer previously, and I didn't want to go down it again. So, this time, I chose to follow the voice of my inner self, which opened me up to love, strength, and courage.

I invite you to open up to your own transformation by dropping your filters and living fearlessly—particularly when you're standing up against the beliefs of others.

Meditation for Tuning In

This meditation will open your channels for receiving guidance. Over time, these voices or downloads will just be a part of you.

"As I sit quietly, I tune in to my inner guidance.
I hear its still, small voice, not audible to human ears.

Sometimes it's not a voice but a visual.

*It communicates in loving snapshots of telepathy, whether in words
or pictures.*

I open myself up and inhale these snapshots into my senses.

I breathe them into my heart and soul.

I feel protected.

I feel loved."

Chapter 8

OPENING TO ABUNDANCE
WITHOUT GUILT

MANTRA:
"It's as important to receive as it is to give."

We can hardly talk about being out in the world, following our calling, and expressing ourselves fully without discussing money. Just the mention of it can trigger sentiments from fear to elation, and often these feelings are quite strong. It's a sensitive subject, the elephant in the room that many of us avoid like crazy. I tend to steer clear of talking about money. First, I'm no expert in the field of finance, and second, if I don't frame my comments about money carefully, the topic can set people off, particularly in spiritual circles (more about that later in the chapter).

However, since we can't survive without money in our physical world, I felt this book wouldn't be complete unless I touched on why it's a trigger for so many. From the letters I receive from the public, a proportionately high number of empathic people struggle with money and have trouble making enough to live, particularly if they're spiritual teachers, involved in the healing arts, or any other service-related, heart-based work.

The dichotomy for empaths is that on the one hand, because we're so in tune with the rhythm of the Universe, we're in the best position to be a powerful channel for money and power to just move through us. We're extremely good at tuning in to our inner wisdom and inner voice, and connecting to all creation. However, we shy away from power and from asking for what we deserve, especially if we were taught that the love of money is the root of all evil or that it's more blessed to give than receive.

In this chapter, we'll explore how to overcome some of the obstacles and beliefs that keep so many empaths stuck in poverty and feelings of scarcity.

As a Society, Our Priorities Are Whacked

Let's start by looking at the larger problem—our greater physical reality beyond our personal spiritual or religious beliefs. Unless you're a hermit, you'll notice that every part of our culture is deeply enmeshed in a relationship with money—a relationship so deep and entangled that we couldn't sever it without heavy casualties. Money is required for pretty much everything we need to live, from our basic necessities of food and shelter all the way to creative freedom. In a nutshell, we can't survive in the modern world without it.

Yet we who live in developed countries have taken our dependency on money to the next level, nearly worshipping money and those in this world who control it (those who control our energy supply; our medical, food, and drug needs; and other critical requirements of life). We've relinquished our power to them, and in turn, they control our world leaders and our mass media, and both end up controlling us. Maybe we've allowed this control to happen because we measure people's worth by how much money they have, and measure success only in terms of financial wealth. In fact, the word "success" has become synonymous with "financial wealth." Possibly this has always been true, and because of the Internet, it's more apparent now, more in our faces.

We sacrifice our own lives chasing our tails, running ourselves to the ground and burning out, just to be able to buy more and own more and more stuff that keeps us feeling (temporarily) successful, until the newer, faster, and shinier models of everything are launched. Though many of us could live on far less, the advertisers play on our fears and insecurities by convincing us we're inadequate and incomplete unless we have the newest car, the latest branded handbag, or the holiday at the just-opened resort in the Bahamas—just to keep us spending our money, which keeps us on a never-ending treadmill of not feeling fulfilled unless we chase after more.

As a result, many of us have made the pursuit of money our number one priority, over and above our health, our relationships, and our moral and spiritual values. (Although—and this is encouraging—opinions may be swinging the other way with millennials, who, as far as their professional life goes, value career development, purposeful work, work/life balance, and company culture more than financial remuneration.[1]) With extreme global financial inequality at an all-time high[2], and 7.7 billion people on the planet as of this writing, we've bought into the perception that there isn't enough money to go around, and that we have to compete with everyone else to get as much as we can, or someone else will get it before we do. This perception has led many people to do things for money that are not only unethical, but downright criminal. Further, many of our corporations are driven by greed (their first obligation being to make a profit for their shareholders), not by service to humanity, to the point that it's actually killing our planet.

We also value money over our time, or simply have to work more hours to make ends meet, so we don't live our lives to the fullest with the time we have.

Here's an example. I was a guest on a radio show when a woman called in. I'd barely said "hello" when she jumped in with, "I'm in a job I hate and it's really draining me, and I dread going to work every day. I don't know what to do! What do I do?"

I suggested to her that she really needed to start loving and valuing herself more. "You might consider cutting down your hours or quitting your job, even if it means taking another one that pays less but that you like more." I could feel her freaking out. "Even if it's just a temporary meas—"

"No," she said. "I can't! If I quit this job I'll lose my insurance, and I won't have any money to meet my mortgage, pay my bills, buy food. Quitting will kill me."

I tried to tell her that by working in the job she hated, she was depleting her life force energy, which might very well kill her as well.

"Okay, thanks," she said, though I could tell she meant anything but, and then she hung up. She couldn't hear what I had to say. She was frightened and in survival mode.

Studies have shown that when we're caught up in survival mode, as this woman was, our executive functioning suffers. We don't have the resources to devote to creative solutions. This is where centering ourselves, breathing, and connecting to the web of consciousness helps to calm our minds, see things in different ways, and spark our creativity. When we calm and open ourselves this way, amazing opportunities come our way. People have told me of jobs appearing out of the blue, financial windfalls coming from unexpected sources, and hobbies that became income streams.

Spirituality and Abundance

Possibly, because of this out-of-whack relationship we have with money, a good many spiritual or religious institutions and teachers insist that "the love of money is the root of all evil" and must be kept *out* of spirituality. Religious holy books are full of admonitions against possessing wealth, and the corrosive influence that money has on our eternal souls. In these circles, money is considered unspiritual and filled with contamination, the nemesis of spirituality. So making a lot of money is a topic that's rarely spoken about in spiritual terms, and making money from doing any form of spiritual work is considered taboo. All spiritual teachings and healings must be offered for free, or by donation, to keep them pure and unsullied by the crass infection of money. Those who charge for healing, service, or spiritual teaching are judged as being unspiritual or greedy, or not to be trusted because they have an agenda.

On the surface, keeping money out of our spiritual institutions may seem like a healthy way to bring balance to our money-crazed culture. However, when taken to the extreme, this thinking just gives the folks with money a different kind of power over us. Remember how I said that empaths are attracted to spirituality like moths to a flame? Empaths are inherently attuned to some of the deeper mysteries of life and make natural spiritual teachers, healers, animal rescuers, environmentalists, educators, peace activists, creative artists, and practitioners of all forms of heart-based work. It's innate to them to use their gifts to help others feel better, and to do so makes them feel better themselves. To expect them not to express their gifts would be like starving them of oxygen.

Now, if you throw into this mix the belief that it's unspiritual to charge money for spiritual or heart-based work, it's no wonder that the people whose very nature it is to do spiritual work sing the anthem of "I want to be of service to others, but I'm struggling to make money doing what I love!"

In other words, our society has created a paradigm that turns a blind eye to corporations that financially flourish to the point of greed (in many cases even employing the services of sweatshops), but we chastise our spiritual teachers and healers for charging money for their heartfelt work, accusing them of not being spiritual.

This thinking just opens the door to empaths being exploited. If our healers and heart-based workers struggle financially and aren't lucky enough to find paid work in a field that honors their sensitive natures, they are forced to heed the corporate call to hustle harder and take on a job that doesn't align with their soul's purpose to pay their bills, only to suffer from burnout a few years later. Even our millennials are being forced to hustle two to three jobs at a time just to pay off their student loans, which is really not the most ideal way to start adulthood.

Shortly after my own journey with cancer and my near-death experience, I knew I had to figure out what to do with the rest of my life. This was when I lived in Hong Kong. I hadn't worked during the four years I was sick, and no part of me wanted to go back to the corporate world I'd left behind. Danny had lost his job because he'd stopped going into work to take care of me—we both thought I was dying. Both of us were deeply affected by what I'd experienced, and our priorities had changed.

Although we were without jobs, we had so much we valued far more than money. I was now healthy, and we were both so grateful that I had another chance at life. I knew I was safe, taken care of, and had no reason to worry, even though we were, at this time, more broke than we'd ever been, and we were living from month to month. I knew there must be a greater reason for me to be sent back! "You have gifts waiting for you on the other side," my dad had said. I was so sure something would unfold.

I started writing about my experience in an online forum, communicating everything I'd learned from my NDE. I got the idea that maybe I was *meant* to share my experience, or teach what I'd learned. I felt excited at the thought, and I just loved the idea that maybe teaching what I'd learned was my purpose.

I talked with a local alternative healing center about renting a room to conduct a small teaching event. I booked the room for a date a few months in the future, and then started planning. I wanted to share everything I'd learned from the other side. I wanted people to know that they are six-sensory beings, and show them how to get in touch with their inner selves. I wanted to teach how to raise our energy together, and that, if someone in the group was going through a health challenge, we could all focus our collective and then individual healing energy on that person.

I created a flier for the event, which I e-mailed to friends and acquaintances, asking them to share it with others. This was in 2008, when social media wasn't the huge presence it is today. I truly was excited about the event, and really felt that maybe I'd just found my purpose—or at least the start of something that would lead to my purpose. Teaching what I'd learned on the other side just felt *so right!* Then my world was turned upside down by a single e-mail from a woman named Brenda who believed she was well-meaning.

Brenda wrote what, to me, felt like a scathing e-mail, in which she framed herself as a "well-wisher," claiming to want only what was best for me, yet she went on to accuse me of exploiting vulnerable people by charging them to come to my event. "How can you live with yourself?" she asked. "How can you charge for your services? Your NDE and everything you learned from it are gifts from God. You're taking advantage of desperate people, particularly those who had cancer, by charging them to come to your event. You should be ashamed."

This is the very thing empaths who offer their gifts as services—especially in the area of spirituality—come up against every day, making it especially difficult to charge what we're worth. My ears burned as her words reverberated loudly inside my head. My heart pounded, as all she wrote cut through me. My bubble had burst, and I felt completely deflated. There was no way I wanted to do anything that could be perceived as exploiting vulnerable people. That was the last thing I'd intended to do. Although I was already doing a lot of teaching for free online, I didn't have enough money to do the event—my little event—for free. The cost of the venue was too high, so I canceled it.

At the time, I didn't see the irony that Brenda was a wealthy, high-flying, corporate lawyer who charged hundreds of dollars for each hour of her time, and lived in a luxurious home. She was working with her God-given gifts as well. (Bear in mind also that Danny and I were, at that point in time, financially struggling and literally living from month to month in a tiny, modest home in a poor, rural village on the periphery of Hong Kong.) While I felt no negativity toward her for what she did for a living or how wealthy she was, I felt judged. She didn't even really know me!

I wasn't out to gouge people. What I was offering helped alleviate people's fear. It offered a different way of viewing their bodies and illness, one where they could see themselves beyond their illness. This view allowed them to focus on getting well because they loved themselves and had a passion for living, as opposed to constantly focusing purely on eradicating dis-ease. I wanted to empower people who were facing illness, and give them hope. At the same time, I was acting responsibly to ensure that I wasn't taking people away from their medical treatments.

Even if what I experienced was a gift from the divine, or the Universe, all I wanted to do was share it with others, while trying to live in this world. Should gifts from our hearts not be rewarded the way we rewarded every other kind of work or service? *I was completely sure* that the things I learned on the other side could help, because those I had already helped online were saying so. But now I felt afraid to go out and teach everything I'd learned from my NDE because I assumed others would feel the same way as Brenda did, especially if I started to earn some kind of a sustainable income from doing this work.

So many empaths tell me they struggle with this same topic. Some fear charging for their services and others have been called out for charging at all, or for raising their prices. Think of teachers. They are seriously underpaid, yet still give their all to their students. But when teachers ask for more, and even go on strike, they're called on the carpet for abandoning the education of the kids in their charge. This is their living. This is how they support their families. If their needs aren't met, there won't be anything left to give to the kids. You must meet your own needs so your light doesn't dim, so you can share it with others.

Seeing Things Differently

To avoid anyone thinking I was exploiting vulnerable people, I decided to take on a part-time corporate consulting job to pay my bills *and* sustain the work that I really wanted to do, the work that came from my soul. When I wasn't working, I could do what I loved—sharing and experimenting with what I'd learned on the other side. I kept writing about my experience, relating what I'd learned—and continued to learn—from it in online forums, and Skyped with people from all over the world whom I met in these forums. I loved what I was doing so much that, over time, I started taking on fewer and fewer consulting gigs, and spending more and more time conducting online healing sessions, meditations, and other energy experiments, helping people to increase their life force energy, giving them hope and strength during their illnesses. I didn't charge for any of this work—I just loved doing it, but because I was now taking on fewer consulting gigs to do what I loved, I wasn't bringing in that much money.

Danny was trying to get a new business idea off the ground, and between us, we weren't making nearly enough to survive, but I kept trying to sweep that under the rug, hoping that if I ignored it, the problem would eventually go away. I kept convincing myself that I came back for a reason, and I knew I was looked after.

But every time we had to pay a bill, I felt a twang of financial fear creeping in. I was watching our savings dwindle down and down. I didn't know how we could go on like this, and I didn't know what to do about it, either. I was torn because I really didn't feel I had come back from the other side just to continue working as a cog in the gears of a large corporate machine again, simply to pay bills. Making money for the sake of money itself held no interest to me.

To make matters worse, I started to feel extremely drained. Since I was doing my healing consultations for free, I attracted a lot of people who wanted to talk to me and get my help, many more people than I could handle. And on top of that, I wasn't resting or taking time for myself. If I rested, I felt guilty because there were people who were sick, and were wanting to talk to me about how to heal from their illness. I became completely burned out, and the fear started to creep back in. I recognized those old emotions that caused my cancer in the first place; the emotion of *fear*, of not being able to be there for everyone; and *guilt* because I had my health and they didn't.

How am I going to continue like this? I wondered. *Am I supposed to just go back to living a life of working in the corporate world, where you're not judged for making money?* In fact, in that world, the more you earn, the more you're admired. But it felt so meaningless to me to have died and come back just to return to a soulless corporation. I didn't know what to do.

The answer came after I'd been struggling with this situation for about two years. I was invited to a dinner hosted by the Hong Kong International Coaching Community. The event included a moving talk by a visiting inspirational speaker named Lenny Ravich, who'd been told about my NDE and wanted to know more. I sat next to him at dinner and shared my story, ending with, "And my dad told me to go and live my life fearlessly! And that's when I came out of the coma, and the cancer healed, and here I am!"

Lenny was beaming at this point, and then asked, "Well, have you?"

I looked bewildered. "Have I what?"

"Lived your life fearlessly?"

"Well . . . more or less."

"What do you mean?" he asked. "Either you have or you haven't."

I told him that I had for the most part but that, for a while now, financial fears had started creeping back into my life.

"You died and came back!" he said. "You had cancer and it's gone. How can you fear *anything* after that, let alone not having enough money?"

I told him about Brenda's letter and my fear of making money from my passion, that I didn't want to seem like I was exploiting vulnerable or sick people.

Lenny looked at me incredulously. "You were sent back for a reason, and your dad told you to live your life fearlessly! How can you go back into that cycle of fear, just because of what this woman said to you? She's part of the very paradigm you broke away from after your cancer healed. Why should you close yourself off from being rewarded by the Universe in whatever way it comes to you, when you're following your heart?" Lenny was fervent and zealous as he expressed this, and his words were having a really deep impact on me.

"Your dad said to live fearlessly," he said again. "He said you would heal, and you did! So how can you not trust him on this? How can you let him down and not live fearlessly, like he asked?"

He was right. I was letting my dad down if I wasn't following my heart and living fearlessly. More important, I was letting myself down. How could I have doubted my dad? I could have hugged Lenny right then. In fact, if I'm not mistaken, I think I did!

As Lenny talked, it almost felt as though my dad were being channeled through him, without Lenny even realizing it. Something deep shifted within me after that conversation, and I reached a whole new level of understanding about my relationship with money.

I realized that if I bought into the belief that it's not spiritual to receive payment for work that's done from the heart, then I'd have to find some other work just to be able to pay my bills. Believing that money is *not* spiritual would force me to find work *away* from my own spirituality, in jobs that for me were soulless, just to be able to earn money to pay our bills, at the expense of my dharma.

Time to Shift Gears!

Once I saw how damaging the belief that money isn't spiritual was for me, I was able to release its hold. As an empath, I knew that no matter how much money I made, I wouldn't be able to live with myself unless

I was helping other people. That goes for most empaths out there, including those of you reading these words. You don't have to worry about falling into the greed trap. As an empath, you'll help people as sure as you'll breathe air. No matter what. It's a given.

I then made the commitment to myself to do only work that came from the heart, because it was important to follow my purpose, to do what energized me, and when I was energized, I was giving my best to others. That was the best form of service I could perform, for myself and for others—to come from that place of excitement and passion. And to keep doing this, I had to allow financial abundance into my life. This shift in thinking opened up a whole new world for me. I started by finally accepting a paid speaking gig at a friend's healing center (she'd been inviting me for some time), and almost immediately after accepting that, Wayne Dyer discovered my story on the Internet and had his publishers track me down—and the rest is history!

It was only when I let go of the fear of judgment from others, driven by their belief that money isn't spiritual, that the world responded by supporting me in what I do. I truly believe that the more we believe in ourselves, and know we're worthy, the more money flows our way. This allows us the freedom to create more and do more, for others, for ourselves, and for the planet.

Guilt is a common issue that empaths face when it comes to making money. They feel guilty about making money when others are struggling, and they feel guilty spending money on themselves while there's hunger and poverty in the world. Once again, this is what makes the empath very good at giving, but terrible at receiving.

On a Facebook Live video, where I was speaking about guilt and money, I addressed comments from an empath who was struggling financially. One of her comments read, "When I get paid, the homeless eat." In other words, the minute she had money, she'd feed anyone who had less than she did, and she was back to being broke again. This was very noble of her, but her life needn't have been such a struggle with not having enough for herself. If she'd been able to spend some on herself, it would have the opposite effect, because the more you love yourself, and believe you're worthy, the more money actually comes to you, and the more you have to share with others. Because, remember, money isn't limited or finite. So much of what comes into our lives depends on how open we are to receiving, and how worthy and deserving we feel.

I was recently interviewed by Brian Rose of *London Real*, in the United Kingdom, and we were talking about empaths, and how hard it was for them to charge money for the work they do. He shared with me a story of one of his students from his Business Accelerator program: "The student was very empathetic, but he always felt bad charging money, and so he always set up his businesses as these non-profit organizations, which ended up ruining him financially," Brian said. "Finally, it even ruined one of his marriages, and when he [started] my course, I said, 'No, no, no. Money isn't bad. Money actually allows you to help more people.' Once he made that switch [in his perception] everything changed, and he became more successful. It's because he was kind of loving himself first."

I'm sure that many of you can identify with the issues this student struggled with, and many may identify with one of the lessons he learned: When you charge what you deserve, you attract people who are happy to pay for your services, and people you enjoy working with.

Going from Icky to Exciting

What's lost on most people is that those corporations that control money, and the empaths who don't charge and who want to do everything for free, are two sides of the same coin. That coin is the belief that there isn't enough to go around. The struggling empaths who martyr themselves may judge greedy corporations, but they're buying into the same belief system of scarcity.

If the pursuit of money is robbing you of your health, your time, your relationships, or your life, then you have become a slave to money, and the money is actually *subtracting* from your life, instead of adding to it. The best service you can do for yourself, and for those around you, is to allow yourself to believe money can be good, so you can be a channel for money to flow through you, and help others.

As the woman wrote during my Facebook Live broadcast, "When I get paid, the homeless eat." Imagine if you got paid a lot. Then more people would eat, and you could take care of yourself, too!

Okay, so how do you get money flowing to you?

1. Recognize that you're an empath and have a tendency to give too much of yourself, without receiving, and a tendency to feel guilty easily—for example, for accepting money for work that comes naturally to you and aligns with your soul's purpose.

2. Get some clarity around your life purpose by asking yourself questions like, *Who am I? What brings me joy? What do I do naturally? What makes me feel alive? What energizes me? What do I always do for free? What could I do every day, without getting burned out?*

3. Open your receiving channels by knowing you're worthy and deserving to be rewarded for following your purpose. Love yourself enough to allow yourself to receive. Love all of yourself, not just your physical body. Love your mind, your spiritual self, the whole of you, including what you can't see.

   Know that there's actually an unlimited amount of money, or abundance, on this planet. This knowledge can be found in ancient wisdom teachings, and today in teachings from Stephen Covey, Dr. Wayne Dyer, Esther Hicks and Abraham, Deepak Chopra, Brené Brown, and Rhonda Bryne (author of

The Secret), just to name a few. I love this ancient Sufi saying: "Abundance can be had by simply receiving what already has been given." In other words, gratitude is a way of opening to abundance. Letting go of our inner restrictions, such as the ones I've discussed in this chapter, is another. As Wayne Dyer wrote, "When you change the way you look at things, the things you look at change. When you see the world as abundant and friendly, your intentions are genuine possibilities."[3]

With that in mind, shed the beliefs that "You have to work hard for your money" or "Money doesn't grow on trees!" or "You shouldn't be charging for spiritual work." The world needs you to survive to share your gift. One method I use and teach is to close your eyes and imagine putting your limiting beliefs (those that are holding you back or weighing you down) into a backpack, which you've strapped to your back, and then removing that backpack and handing it to a spirit guide, whoever you choose—Buddha, Jesus, a guardian angel, archangel, or ascended master—whoever is standing right in front of you, and they're saying to you, "Give me that backpack. Give me that backpack. You don't have to wear it anymore. It's mine. I've taken that load off you. You're free and clear. You are now clear to express the divine. You are now free and clear." I do this every morning—hand off the pack.

4. Be aware that being an empath is a gift, and start to think of yourself as a channel for money to flow through you, rather than a dam blocking that flow. Think about what you'd spend it on. How would you take care of yourself to make sure your energies are charged? How would you help others? What would you do for the world if you had money just flowing in? Don't be afraid to dream big. Don't let the fear of not having money limit your dreams.

5. Now this is the tricky part: After you let the first four points sink in, take your focus *off* money and onto your purpose. Make that purpose your priority in life. Focus on what you're here to do, your dreams for yourself and the planet, and how to increase your energy. If you don't have a purpose yet, focus on increasing your life force energy by doing things that make you feel joyful and by learning to receive.

6. When the money does start to come in, allow yourself to enjoy receiving it! Keep those feelings of guilt in check; your being poor isn't going to help others. The best way to be a clear channel for more to come in is to be grateful, and lovingly receive the money that does come in.

7. If your tendency is to use all your money to help others, or to take care of your loved ones while neglecting yourself, it's time to change that habit and put some aside for your own self-care and pleasure. Spend (even a part of it) on yourself without guilt. Doing so reinforces within you that you're deserving and worthy of the money, and it also reinforces that you're trusting more will come in.

8. As your business or career starts to thrive, learn to *love* this vehicle, and realize that your business or career loves *you*. Many of us who do heart-based work have a tendency to feel *icky* about money and business, believing that it gets in the way of our real purpose. Or we think of running our business as a chore, something that just has to be done, even though it's no fun. When I changed my perspective about that, my business started to flourish even more!

That shift happened when I realized that my business takes care of me. It provides me with the resources I need to take care of myself, my extended family, and my team, so that we can be out there doing what we do for the world. Because my business takes care of me, I realized it loves me, which in turn, caused me to value my business, and see it as something more than just a chore, or something icky to be dealt with. Since then, I've actually started to really enjoy seeing it grow, and enjoy my business meetings with my team, as well as my accountants, to see how I can continue to make my business grow, and impact the world and lives of others even more. It's exciting.

I encourage you to try these steps. They work! The idea is to take the ickiness out of the topic of money, and treat money as what it is—merely a tool that provides for and nourishes you and your loved ones while you go out into the world to be all you can be. The more you can reinforce that belief within yourself, the more you open the channel to receive abundance from the Universe.

It feels good to view money as a sign that you're on the right path, you're in the flow. And if the money isn't coming in the way you'd like, it's not that you're on the wrong path, it may just not be time. If you have passion for what you're doing, keep at it!

Stepping into Your Power

This chapter has been one of the hardest for me to write. However, I feel it's an important topic to tackle because unless we get a handle on our financial needs, our lives will be ruled by money—or the lack thereof. I see money as merely a tool, a form of energy that serves us and nurtures us and those we work with while we exercise our soul's purpose. For me, it nurtures me and my team, while I'm in service to the world.

It's my belief and hope that as empaths start to earn money they deserve and take positions of power and leadership both in the workplace and in society, we'll begin to see more financial equality in the world, a balancing, and a shift in the way we view money. To me, empaths and sensitive people are the ones most likely to bring balance to the disparity that currently exists. It's critical for us to dig deep, and find the courage to step into our own power.

How do you do this? First you develop your internal power and sense of knowing by immersing yourself in the concepts presented in this book. Then reach out externally by speaking up, sharing your thoughts and ideas—express yourself from that place of knowing, confidence, and self-love. And from that place, make the conscious decision to act, to step up, to lead—to claim your power rather than relinquish it.

In the workplace, whether you run your own business or work in a group environment, your path to claiming your power and expressing it is the same, no matter what position you hold. Share your opinions, contribute to solutions, come from a place of love. If you come from that place of inner strength and rely on your strong intuition about people and situations, you'll be surprised at the freedom that it brings. I'm not saying you'll always be heard, or get your way, but you'll start creating that inner freedom and outer expression that are so critical to being a greater force in the world. And remember, if you feel stifled in one job or with one client, you can change jobs. You can let that client go, with love.

It's crucial that we stop waiting for others to approve of us, or give us "permission" to act. We need to claim our sense of worth, with the knowledge that our own permission is enough. This is key. I want empaths to be more successful. I would love to see more empaths thrive so that the world can be a better place for more people, instead of the wealth being controlled by a very few. I believe that to be true. It's imperative for empaths to believe in ourselves and claim our power. I urge you to step forward.

Part of stepping forward and claiming your power is to pay attention to where you're putting money as a priority over other, more important areas of your life. For example, your relationships, your time, this planet we live on, the air we breathe—all these are things that people currently sacrifice for money. I believe our lives would be much richer if we lived with that priority reversed. Think what a huge shift that would be.

As you learn to step into your own power, as you face the challenges that come with putting yourself out there and becoming more powerful—people who may try to take advantage of you, disagree with your philosophy about money, and give you a hard time for charging or earning too much for what you do—keep stepping into your power and moving forward. I wouldn't trade what I've been through for anything because I'm finding that the more I move forward in my chosen direction, the more I'm stepping into a position where I can help even more people, which is one of my greatest pleasures—to help as many people as possible. Your calling might be to cook for others, teach, write, act, or work in the healing arts. As you step into your power, you'll find that you can reach more people and enjoy an overflow of abundance, with more than enough to give to others.

What if we changed the parameters a bit, and instead of giving money all our power and making it our number one priority, we decided that our health, or our life force energy, was going to be our number one priority? What if we made the amount of life force energy we had at our disposal our number one priority for measuring success? How would this change the quality of our life?

If money lost its hold over us, our lives and the world would change dramatically. Priorities would change. To me, it starts with shifting the parameters of what "success" means, and reversing the belief that we live in a world of scarcity where there isn't enough to go around. It means coming from a place of gratitude for what we have, valuing our unique skills and our contribution to society, and expressing ourselves freely and joyfully. Knowing we are all connected, and feeling that connection, opens the flow of our own divinity.

Meditation for Abundance

By repeating these words, you open the channels for the abundant flow
of giving and receiving.

> *"I am supported in every way,*
> *including financially.*
> *As I share my gifts with the world,*
> *I open myself up to receiving,*
> *knowing that I am worthy of abundance.*
> *I allow myself to be a channel for abundance to flow through me,*
> *so that it may replenish me, and allow me to serve all those I*
> *reach."*

Chapter 9

SAYING "YES" TO SAYING "NO"

MANTRA:
"It's okay to love myself enough to say 'no.' "

Opening to our divinity means honoring that divinity within us. It can be a challenge. If you're anything like I am, then I suspect you have trouble saying "no," even when you *really* don't want to do something. Not all empaths have trouble turning someone down, but it's common for us because we sense the feelings of those around us and often feel the emotional needs of others stronger than our own. While the empath's love of being of service is a good thing, you have to ask yourself whether that act of service is increasing your life force energy or depleting it. In other words, are you saying "yes" out of a real desire to say "yes," or are you saying "yes" because you feel you *should* be saying it to fulfill your duty or obligation?

We empaths seem to think we're doing a service when we sacrifice our own needs by saying "yes" when we'd rather not. But our reluctance to say "no" causes us to either make excuses rather than being straightforward, or end up doing things we don't want to do because we can't say "no." The former is dishonest, and the latter ends up depleting us, so we end up drained, overstretched, and in some cases, ill. We subsequently drain those around us, especially those who care for us deeply. The more sensitive we are, the more likely we are to feel shame, guilt, and discomfort when we disappoint others. So our drive to please others, as I've said, is twofold: a need to alleviate the problems of others because we feel what they feel, and a need to avoid the pain of feeling guilty if we disappoint them or fail to meet their expectations.

Subjugating your needs for a long period of time to help fulfill the needs of those who don't care about your needs leads to resentment and repressed anger. A 2013 study by the Harvard T.H. Chan School of Public Health and the University of Rochester showed that people who bottled up their emotions increased their chance of premature death from all causes by more than 30 percent, and their risk of cancer by 70 percent.[1] So how do empaths navigate close relationships? And what are the pitfalls for those in a relationship with us? Being in a relationship can be tough for both partners. Empaths need a lot of alone time, our own physical space, and a quiet environment. We can unintentionally sabotage relationships by becoming a people-pleaser, compromising our boundaries, and subjugating ourselves to our partners. We're also extremely giving, understanding, sensitive to the needs of others, and supportive.

If we're around someone who doesn't understand empaths and won't honor our needs, we can lose ourselves, or in an attempt to keep the peace, sacrifice those needs, and then we're in trouble. If we're with someone whose needs are very different from our own fundamental needs—maybe they like to be together 24/7, love to socialize, love background noise, and love constant conversation—that will be tough for both parties. Recognizing and respecting these differences can go a long way toward creating healthy, workable compromises.

The relationships we want to steer clear of are with those whose primary concern is themselves. Narcissists are especially attracted to us, because we see the true self behind the masks they show the world and want to love and nurture that person. And they desperately want that unconditional love and nurturing. But the minute we cross them—disagree, or find fault, or do anything that threatens their shaky yet inflated sense of self—we can lose ourselves completely to avoid their disapproval and the withholding of their affection.

When two empaths come together, the heart connection, mutual understanding, and ability to feel what the other is feeling can result in a soul-deep, profound relationship. On the downside, each partner picks up the other's emotional and physical distress. And there isn't much room for secrets; the other always knows what you're feeling or aren't saying.

Relationships are a spiritual connection and must be treated with love and understanding by both parties. So it's extremely important for empaths and their friends to express their needs and preferences and find a way to honor both. Communication, love, and respect can go a long way to building a strong foundation and a lasting relationship.

Tripping on Guilt

Guilt is the primary reason we subvert ourselves to others. For empaths, guilt can be pervasive. It's part of the reason why we have trouble saying no. One of the biggest reasons I couldn't say no was because of the guilt I felt if I disappointed someone or let them down. I was constantly weighing which was worse: doing what I didn't want to do, or the guilt from saying "no." For example, when I was in my early twenties and single, my friend Tanisha, a single mother with young children, was struggling to make ends meet while taking care of her two school-age kids. She really wanted to date again but had no time in her busy schedule to do anything but work and care for her children. I really felt for her, and I mean deeply! In my mind, I put myself in her situation—as empaths naturally do—and felt how hard it would be to be in her shoes. I didn't like how I felt, so I made it my mission to help her because I *needed* for her to feel better; I often took care of her kids while she went out or helped her where I could.

However, over time, her situation didn't improve, and she became really comfortable with our arrangement. I, on the other hand, started to feel taken for granted. I felt that she saw me as a permanent solution to her problems. Being a single young woman myself, I, too, had needs and desires, and I slowly started to feel that mine were being subverted so she could get hers met. I can't blame Tanisha, because this is a pattern that empaths run into frequently. We attract needy people and make them feel so comfortable that they have no incentive to change their situation.

We convince ourselves that this is what friends do for one another, even though, deep down, we know we wouldn't feel comfortable asking this from others because of our difficulty receiving. The problem is, the longer the situation goes on, the harder it becomes to extricate ourselves from the situation, leading to larger consequences that could have been avoided or addressed much earlier. In Tanisha's case, my resentment built until we had a huge argument that was out of proportion to what triggered it. After things settled down, though, I was the one who apologized for exploding because the trigger didn't warrant the anger I'd expressed. Not only was the original issue still unresolved, but I felt guilty for being angry and resentful toward her. My feelings caused me to judge myself, beat myself up, and believe I was being a crappy friend. I then doubled down on trying to be a good friend, which caused me to feel more resentment toward her for taking up all my time and attention. This pattern of resentment-exploding-and-guilt-doubling-down seemed to be standard issue for many situations in my life. Finding ourselves in this type of lose-lose situation is a common occurrence for empaths. What a crazy way to live, and expend energy.

The situation finally came to a head when I met and fell in love with my husband, Danny. We were dating and spending a lot of time with each other, and I noticed that Tanisha wasn't happy for me. I was surprised. I thought she would be ecstatic that I was with a man who made me happy. But I no longer had as much time for her, and she was starting to resent Danny. I found myself bending over backward, trying to appease her. Still, many times I felt she put me in a position of choosing between her and Danny, instead of just welcoming him into my life, which would have been the healthy thing to do.

Of course, I chose Danny, and with a lot of pain, grief, and guilt in my heart, I walked away from the friendship. I was only able to see it for what it was in hindsight. After some time, Tanisha came back into my life and even apologized, but only when she saw I wasn't coming back and was truly happy without her in my life.

Looking back on my misguided friendship with Tanisha, and other such events in my life, I realize that being nonconfrontational and trying to avoid conflict at all costs actually leads to even more conflicts in the long run. We avoid confrontation because we fear that it's going to deplete us. But if we can become fearless about standing up for ourselves, and do it in the kindest way possible, it will become easier, and we'll feel a strong sense of self-love that comes from taking care of ourselves. Had I listened to my heart much earlier and spoken up, it would have been painful, but it would have saved me a lot of heartache later.

Saying No to Unhealthy Relationships

When we're afraid of disappointing people, we end up being what they want us to be. This fear of disappointment keeps us dancing for others. I now know that when I say "no" to unhealthy relationships, I'm actually opening the space for healthy relationships to come in or, as sometimes happens, for the person with whom I have the unhealthy relationship to realize the value of our relationship and work at making it healthier.

I would like to add a little piece of advice here: Don't wait or hope for others to change. I did that with Tanisha for years, and it didn't happen. As long as we continue to be doormats, there's no incentive for others to change. I had to walk away. If you're in a one-sided relationship and decide to walk away, the other person may promise to make changes, but don't count on it. And if they don't make changes, it means that the relationship exists only if you are their doormat. If that's not what you want, then keep walking. The hardest part is not acquiescing if they do come after you again with the promise of change. In my case, Tanisha was forced to change because she was aware of how in love Danny and I were, so she was careful not to push me away or put me in a position to choose between him or her when it came to where to spend my time or my energy.

The need to have everyone feel good before you can feel good is an even bigger issue if you are in a dysfunctional or codependent relationship, where your partner may be a bottomless well of needs. I'm so grateful that Danny is as sensitive to my needs as I am to his. I couldn't wish for anyone more suitable for someone like me, and I know he feels the same way.

One of the things I loved about Danny right from the start was that he encouraged me to say "no" if I didn't feel like doing something. He always wanted me to be authentic and express what I truly felt, and he wouldn't judge me at all, no matter what. He never wanted me to do anything that didn't feel right for me, just to please him, and he would always remind me of that, because he was aware that I had a tendency to do that. I felt loved unconditionally by him. But with others, I could never say "no." Even when I had cancer, I still found it hard. Death finally cured me of that affliction, and I lost many friends, including Tanisha, after my NDE, because I no longer sacrificed myself for them. Looking back, I know that the cancer was my body's way of fighting back against my inability to say "no."

Before I died, I seemed to attract needy people, like Tanisha. Needy people are drawn to empaths because someone who is less empathic would walk away from such a one-sided relationship. But empaths stay, often because we feel guilty if we can't rescue or help those in need. That dynamic was exhausting. I was either getting worn down trying to fulfill the never-ending requirements of others, or feeling guilty for walking away. Being in this lose-lose situation is a nightmare for the empath.

Hay House, my previous publisher, ran a radio station for their authors, on which I had a weekly show. I once received a call on my radio show from a woman named Loraine. She'd heard me share the story of my experience with Tanisha, which prompted her to call to tell me about a similar situation with her boss Ben. "It was my dream job," she said of her project manager position with a marketing firm. "I was determined to do everything I could to prove I was the best person for the job and excel. I wanted everyone to know, including my boss, and to be honest, myself, that I was extremely qualified. From my very first day, I went all out—anticipating every need; submitting reports, complete with pivot tables; completing all projects ahead of time and under budget; staying late. Throughout the day, my mantra was, *What else can I do? How can this be better? How can I make Ben's life easier?* Instead of working 9:00 to 5:30, I'd get to work 7:30 every morning and leave at 8:00. I didn't care. I loved the work. But I became addicted to the frenzy, the striving, to seeing Ben smile or nod with approval. And I felt so guilty if I missed one small detail, or left earlier than the others, especially him."

Of course Ben got used to this, so when Loraine met the love of her life and started dating, and would often leave the office at a reasonable time, 6:30, to be with her new boyfriend, Ben started making snide remarks about her leaving "early." "You sure tore out of here last night," he'd say, or "Must be nice." This was ridiculous because she still started her workday at 7:30 and always ate lunch while she worked. Things came to a head when, just a couple of evenings before she called my radio show, Loraine shut down her computer to leave at 6:30 and Ben said in an irritated tone, "Next time you plan to leave early, you need to let me know, so I can give you my reports earlier to work on."

"I snapped," Lorraine said. "For the first time ever. He just looked so smug, so self-righteous. 'Next time you want me to work late, *you* let *me* know!' And then I marched off to the elevator."

She felt great. For about five minutes. Then she felt guilty for snapping, for not being there for Ben. She also worried about losing her job. The following morning, she made sure to be super nice to Ben, to make it up to him. She started working late again, even though she knew she couldn't keep going like this. "There I was again," she said, "caught in the loop of doing better, being faster, being best."

During our call, I told her that she really needed to talk to Ben in an honest way, and tell him that she had a personal life, and that it was just not sustainable for her to spend so many hours at work every day. She really needed to be up-front, and let her boss know that it wasn't working for her, and then see what he said, and if he was unreasonable, she needed to consider looking for another job. I asked her to call into my radio show again, to let me know what happened.

Two weeks later, I got a call from Loraine, and sure enough, she'd confronted Ben. The good news? He admitted he'd felt awful, too, the night she'd snapped at him, and he realized he had been taking advantage of her good nature. He also told her that he really valued her, and was happy that she was in a relationship. She said talking to him and being honest was the best thing she could have done, and wished she had done it earlier, instead of letting the resentment build up. And the bonus is, she now knows how much her boss values her! And even better, she values herself.

The litmus test for determining if you're in the right relationship or situation (such as a job) is to ask yourself, *Am I doing all these things for my friend/colleagues, boss, partner because I truly desire to help them because I love and care for them (or, in a working environment, like and respect them) and they genuinely need my help? Or is it because I feel I should do it, to be a good person, and I don't want to be judged by them and deal with the guilt later?* If it's the latter, then you're not being honest with that person.

Imagine if everything your friend or partner did for you was for the same reason—they felt obligated or fearful of being judged as a bad person. How would you feel if you knew they were only doing things for you because they felt they *should*? Or that they resented you for what they were doing for you? If that were the case and you found out, it would certainly make *you* feel guilty, or hurt.

Another question you might ask yourself is, *Am I afraid to talk to them about my feelings of guilt and obligation?* In other words, can you gently let them know that you can't keep providing help like this, and what it's doing to you? If you're afraid of talking to your friend or partner about how you're really feeling, and you'd rather let the resentment build up than discuss it, then it's not a healthy relationship, and most likely won't end well. Also, if you feel they'll walk away from you unless you continue to acquiesce in the relationship, then that's not a healthy relationship to stay in either.

If you're *questioning* yourself about whether this is a good relationship or not, then something doesn't feel quite right, and that feeling needs to be addressed. If you're too afraid to address it with the person, then the relationship is definitely not right for you. Again, imagine if it were the other person who had these questions in their head about you that you're now having about them? How would you feel? If it would make you feel awful that they would think that way about you, remember: That's what you're currently thinking about them! So you aren't being totally honest with them, nor with yourself within this relationship.

When you're in a relationship with someone you truly care about, even when you're going through a really hard time—maybe your partner is deathly ill or facing a difficult situation—you still know in your heart that there's nowhere else you want to be except with this person. You know that, even if you had to be away doing something else, all you could think of would be what they were going through. But if your spouse, partner, or friend is suffering and you're feeling, *Boy, I really wish I didn't have to do this! I'm always the one stuck helping them, while everyone else gets away. I probably* should *stay because I don't want to deal with their judgment later, but I wish I could be somewhere else or with someone else,* then you're definitely in the wrong relationship.

For example, the way I feel right now about Danny, I know that if he were going through something—whether physical or traumatic or whatever—I wouldn't want to leave his side. I'd go to any length to help him through it, and there would be no guilt or obligation from me, because I love him, and his happiness means the world to me. And if I needed a break to recharge my batteries, I'd be able to tell him easily, because he's empathic enough to understand my needs, too. We're so aware of each other's needs and emotions that we don't weigh each other down. We encourage each other to do what feels right and makes us happy, and we can talk about these things with each other freely, with no fear that the other will be disappointed or walk out of the relationship. We each want what's best for the other, and what makes the other happy.

When I was going through cancer, Danny was there for me 110 percent, and at no time did I feel as though it was an obligation on his part. He made sure I knew there was nowhere else he wanted to be except by my side. If that's not how you and your friend or partner feel about each other, it's better to be honest rather than just be there out of obligation.

Dealing with the Guilt that Accompanies Saying "No"

Now that you understand the importance of saying "no," it's necessary to learn how to deal with the guilt that might arise as a result. As I've said, guilt seems to be one of the biggest reasons that people say "yes" when they mean "no." We sacrifice our self, our health, our well-being out of guilt for others—especially those of us who are women and mothers. Everyone else's needs seem to come first—husband, children, friends, the homeless person down the road.

Empaths feel guilty when we create boundaries to protect ourselves, even from those who hurt us. We often feel guilty judging hurtful people, which then makes it difficult to protect ourselves from those who are potentially harmful.

We also can feel guilty when we're happy, or when things are going well for us. Even when we've done nothing wrong, haven't hurt anyone, and our happiness or success is honestly earned, we feel guilty. We feel guilty for feeling good. Wow! This is misplaced guilt; empaths need to be reminded frequently that their success and good fortune is well earned and well deserved.

After a lot of trial and error, I've come up with helpful tools to deal with guilt that have worked for me:

1. Acceptance and awareness. This means being aware of the shadow side of being an empath (the fear, misplaced guilt, self-denial), and making friends with it. Stop judging yourself for feeling guilty or for being supersensitive, or wanting to please, and learn to accept these traits as the flip side of your gifts.

2. Choose the better option. When in that familiar lose-lose situation, trapped between taking care of yourself and feeling guilty for letting someone down—*feel* into both situations. Visualize both to see which one feels even slightly better, or more authentic. Even if you're left with the guilt, it may well feel better than being a doormat and ignoring what you need.

3. If you're left with a residue of guilt after trying what I've outlined in the first two points, become the observer. Start to observe your misplaced guilt, your agility at avoiding conflict, and the lengths you go through to do so. Then observe your own feelings and emotions, as though you've stepped out of your body.

Notice what you're feeling in your body and where you're feeling it. Notice the common themes in your life that trigger these feelings. Find the patterns. Observe yourself as though you're watching someone else. I've found it easier to do this since my NDE, but I think anyone can do this with practice. It reduces the physical impact that these emotions have on our bodies. It reduces that heavy, stressful, fearful feeling.

4. Develop some gentle language that works for you when you want to say "no." This will help you with conflict resolution. Chances are, if you're like I am, you hate conflict. So to avoid it, here are some things I say when people ask me something I don't want to say "yes" to, at least not right away:

- Let me think about that and come back to you.
- I need to ponder that. Is it okay if I don't make a decision right away?
- I'm really touched that you came to me with this, but I have too much on my plate right now, so as an act of self-care, I'm going to have to turn you down.
- I've thought about it, and now isn't a good time for me, but thank you for thinking of me.

5. Learn to receive! I know, I know—I can't stress receiving enough. Become aware of your difficulty with receiving and open up your receiving channels. See yourself receiving gifts and abundance. See yourself receiving love. See yourself receiving your kindness to yourself by standing up for what you believe, for saying "no" when you want to say "no." You need to receive so you can charge your batteries; so you can be true to yourself and say "no"; so you don't tie yourself in knots to avoid letting anyone down; so you can continue to be a force for good on this planet.

6. Journal. I find writing about my feelings is very cathartic for me and releases a lot of pent-up emotions. Also, with journaling, you become the observer, as outlined in Step 3, so you're helping yourself to desensitize from the emotions; plus, you can read back what you wrote weeks or months later and see how far you've come.

7. And finally, but extremely important, love yourself through this. Don't beat up on yourself! Love yourself more, and laugh at yourself. Laugh at your traits, and don't take yourself so seriously. Laugh at your guilt about saying "no." Laugh about all that goes through your head before you turn someone down or want to turn someone down. Talk about these traits—the rats' nest of tangled feelings involved with aversion to confrontation; fear of failing or disappointing others; and the guilt, guilt, guilt—freely with others. They'll find it refreshing. A sure sign that you love and accept yourself is when you can talk about these traits and they're no longer hot-button issues for you. Know that you're a powerful person, but you could be even more effective if you didn't judge yourself so harshly or let misplaced guilt get the better of you.

These seven points can not only help you manage and deal with misplaced guilt, they can also help to reduce the anxious, stressful, even painful feelings that come with guilt or conflict avoidance.

I cannot stress enough how impactful the simple act of becoming more sensitive to your own inner guidance and learning to say "no" to what doesn't feel right for you can be to changing your life for the better. This ability alone makes you more authentic and allows you to create a life that truly reflects who you are!

Meditation for Saying "No"

You may find yourself whispering these words to yourself on the fly, while finding the courage to say "no."

> *"I honor myself by tuning in to my inner guidance.*
> *I allow myself to say no without guilt.*
> *Saying no does not make me a bad person. On the contrary, it*
> *   makes me a more authentic person.*
> *Letting go of all that is not me*
> *   allows me to set myself free,*
> *   and fully embrace the me who finally emerges."*

Chapter 10

BREAKING THROUGH
GENDER NORMS

MANTRA:
"I embrace my gender."

We've been in a male dominant paradigm for far too long, and we're seeing the repercussions of suppressed feminine energy (the quality of energy both men and women hold), so it's time to swing the pendulum the other way to create balance.

Women who are empaths might follow the status quo to avoid feeling guilty, the disapproval of others, and letting someone else down. Men who are empathic also suffer, but more from a reverse gender bias—they're not "masculine" enough.

I grew up in a cultural environment where I faced tremendous gender disparity. I believed that women were inferior to men, and I carried that belief with me well into adulthood. It's part of our Indian cultural paradigm that women have to be looked after by men because we're too vulnerable, too *sensitive*. It starts out with being looked after by our fathers, and we're expected to stay at home with our parents until we get married, and then let our husbands look after us.

As an adult, before I was married, if I went out in the evenings with my women friends, I had to be accompanied by a male chaperone—my brother or someone my family knew and trusted. All household chores were assigned to me and not my brother. When I would ask my parents why he didn't have to help with the washing up or the cooking, they would say, "Because you're a girl, and he's a boy." In terms of leadership, I was raised to believe the same thing—men were leaders, and if women vied for positions of power or leadership, they'd be considered undesirable to men. Doctors, government figures, news anchors: These were all jobs for men. The supporting roles—assistants, secretaries, nurses— these were for women only.

If you were raised in a similar culture, think about the messages this sent. Think about the kinds of beliefs this forms within us: that we need to be protected by men all the time—which makes us doubt our own abilities as women to think, react, create—to be all that we can be. It makes us doubt our own strength. It makes us doubt our confidence in our own emotions and our own reactions.

This gender bias actually exists in all cultures. Many people say that in Western culture, particularly in American culture, women have nothing to complain about; that we are very free and very liberated from all these beliefs. And that is true to an extent, but only to an extent.

After all, in the United States, until 1973, women couldn't apply for a credit card or a loan without their father's or husband's signature. They could be the top wage-earner in their family, but it didn't matter. Scratch the surface, and I don't believe all that much has changed. We still make $.80 on the dollar, and closer to $.49 if you factor in what we lose in raises and promotions because we take more breaks to take care of family and loved ones.[1] We often lack the confidence needed to rise to positions of leadership, even if we're more qualified than our male colleagues. I always think of the famous Hewlett Packard internal report where women apply for a job only if they met 100 percent of the qualifications, but men apply when they meet only 60 percent.

And while there's global progress worldwide, there's still a huge gender gap. The World Economic Forum's Global Gender Gap Report states that, at the current rates, the overall global gender gap will close in 61 years in Western Europe, 70 years in South Asia, and 165 years in North America."[2] In my opinion, the gap is closing much too slowly.

This kind of conditioning and these cultural beliefs can be hard to overcome, and can lead to even more false beliefs such as "I don't matter," "I'm not good enough," "I'm not worthy unless I have a powerful man by my side," "Married women are more valuable than single women," and so on. Our cultural gender biases and restrictions are filters rather than truths. Outside our 3D reality there is no gender bias, because there is no gender—just energy, which is neither masculine nor feminine. Gender is a part of our biology on this planet, for the purpose of reproduction. By recognizing this point, we can more clearly see gender biases and restrictions for the false filters they are, and help ourselves and others break free of them.

The Runaway Bride

While breaking free can be tough, it's much easier when we come from a place of power. That power comes from being who we truly are. When we rebel against the biases that come with these filters, without self-love and the strength, conviction, and peace with ourselves that comes with it, breaking free can be extremely painful.

I've mentioned that the primary cultural expectation for me was to become a good wife to a suitable husband whom my parents selected for me. That person needed to be part of the same culture, the same heritage, and on the same socioeconomic level. Ultimately, the most important thing I could do was to make myself attractive to men. I carried this conditioning with me until I died. Sadly, because women have less value in traditional Indian society if they're single, the hunt for a mate begins early.

When I was barely a tween, my parents began to groom me to become a good wife for a prospective husband. That meant learning to be subservient, submissive, obedient, desirable, and good at housework. It also meant that I couldn't work or study unless my prospective husband *and* his family permitted it, because according to traditional Indian culture, you don't just marry the man, you marry into the whole family and live with his parents and siblings. The result is that women obey their fathers until they get married and then they obey their husbands—for the rest of their lives.

This life always terrified me. It felt like emotional death. I wanted to be my own person, with the freedom to find work I was passionate about. I also wanted to travel the world, pursue big dreams, and make my own money. I wanted to find my *own* path. The last thing I wanted to do was get married to someone chosen for me. I was a hopeless romantic who wanted to fall in love and be swept off my feet by someone *I* personally chose.

I watched as some of my closest Indian girlfriends got married one after the other (one at seventeen and another at nineteen!). Most of them actually looked forward to getting married, even if it was to a man chosen by their parents within the narrow range of what was permitted. As friends donned their wedding attire, people would ask my parents why their daughter was still single, implying that no one wanted me. I started to doubt myself even more when I noticed that my own girlfriends, who were similar to me, weren't doubting the status quo; in fact, they were excited about something that felt terrifying to me.

This was the onset of a pattern that would take decades to break. I began to second-guess my inner self and assume there truly was something wrong with me. My inability to claim my own personal path and power at the time left me feeling lonely, misunderstood, and scared that I'd end up all alone in life. I vacillated between the need for self-expression and the desire to appease my family; to say "yes" when I meant "no" to the world around me; and to withdraw from my own spotlight instead of stepping into it.

Finally, in my twenties, I agreed to an arranged marriage, only to turn around and do something that was even more wild and shocking than spraying my hair pink in the early '80s. At the last minute, just before the wedding took place—with my inner voice shouting in my head, *Do not go through with this! This is not who you are! This is not who you came here to be!*—I ran away.

The wedding was scheduled to take place in Bombay, and it was to be an elaborate affair, with relatives from all over the world who'd flown in to attend. Venues were booked, as were vendors—photographers, caterers, musicians, and so on. As is the case with Indian weddings, there were at least seven functions lined up. Bailing on this wedding was a very hard decision to make, but I saw no other choice. I'd been engaged to my fiancé for eight months, and had spent those months trying to be everything his family wanted me to be. During that time, I had to seek my fiancé's and his parents' approval on all my decisions—big and small—from choice of clothes to wear on a daily basis to what to learn to cook after we were married. I was worn out by the time our wedding came along. To top it off, because of my fiancé's and in-laws' views, I wouldn't be allowed to work outside the home, earn my own money, travel, or live any of my dreams.

Getting married in this situation would be like going from the frying pan into the fire. As I noted, in an Indian arranged marriage, you don't just marry the man—you inherit a whole new family. My role as a daughter-in-law to my fiancé's parents was an integral part of this alliance, especially since I would have to live with them, and it seemed as though my in-laws were even stricter than my dad!

Three days before the wedding, unable to calm the storm raging in my heart, I decided to confide in my mother. I told her that after eight months, I'd hardly gotten to know my fiancé. His parents had factored into my life far more than he had, training me to be the perfect Indian wife, teaching me how to cook his favorite dishes, and how to dress in Indian clothes. The thought of spending my wedding night with a man I barely knew frightened me like nothing else ever had.

Like a true heroine, my mother hugged me and comforted me, and told me that she wouldn't force me to go through with it. On the one hand, I was relieved. On the other, I was horrified by the thought of how my in-laws would react, and all the guests and relatives who had flown in; not to mention that we still had to deal with the venues, vendors, and everything else! My mom said she'd take care of everything, including speaking with my fiancé and in-laws, making sure that all the relatives and wedding guests were told and compensated, as well as the venues and vendors. She took matters into her hands completely, and only chastised me for not confiding in her earlier.

As expected, when my mother spoke with my fiancé and my in-laws, they were livid, and accused my mother of spoiling me. A huge argument broke out, with them telling my mother to slap me and force me to turn up at the temple on the wedding day. My mother said she would do no such thing.

I didn't have the stomach to stay and watch their reaction. I also knew they would come looking for me, so I ran away and hid at the home of my best friend, who had gone through an arranged marriage at the age of nineteen, which she regretted, and was now dealing with the repercussions. She lived in Bombay at the time, and opened her home to me.

My fiancé's family showed up at the door of my friend's home looking for me, but I hid in the bedroom while she fielded them. I couldn't leave her house, because they were stalking me outside the building, on the street, suspecting that I was there. I stayed there for a month, until all the heat died down, and the last of the overseas relatives flew back home.

Running away from the altar might seem like a courageous move to some people, but in many ways, it came right out of the empath's guidebook. Because I didn't have the courage to say "NO"—because I didn't want to disappoint people or create conflict—I went into denial and agreed to an arranged marriage. But when the actual moment came for me to tie the proverbial knot, I bailed, which created even *more* disappointment and conflict—exactly what I wanted to avoid by acquiescing to everyone in the first place. Either way you sliced it, I was stuck in an untenable situation. And the ensuing uproar brought shame to my family and to the groom's.

When my mother's parents had started to force her down the road of an arranged marriage, she vowed that if she ever had a daughter of her own she would never impose the same restrictions. When she went through with it and married my dad, she had to stifle her true self, but she never got mad at me for not wanting to do the same, or challenged my rebellious streak. In the end, she even sided with me when I ran away. Our extended family accused her of spoiling me, too, because she didn't chastise me or make it hard for me to return home, so that I'd be forced to go back to my husband-to-be. She walked a fine line: trying to garner my dad's approval *and* be present for me. She never blamed or judged me, even when it felt like the whole world, including my dad, was against me. She defended me to the world and stood by my side, dancing between our cultural boundaries and my dreams.

Although my mom never withheld her approval, my dad certainly did. I would have to work really hard to win his, and once I'd won it, I was very temporary. Therefore, I did all I could to maintain it, bending myself out of shape if I had to. And then when I'd lose his approval again, I always felt it was my fault, and believed I'd done something wrong to hurt him. Any little thing could trigger his disapproval and withholding of love—my putting up a life-size poster of a male pop star on my bedroom wall or talking on the phone with a friend late into the night. It was all just regular teenage stuff, but my dad's reactions to these sorts of things were over-the-top. He would lose his temper not only with me, but also my mom, accusing her of indulging me. His anger made me feel guilty, and I'd go through the whole cycle of contorting myself out of shape, trying everything possible to be a good daughter, to win his approval again.

And so it came to pass that when I crossed a line—when I stayed out later than I was allowed, or dated boys who weren't from our culture, or dressed in a fashion that was even mildly provocative—my dad would get mad at me and my mom. That made me feel awful and even more conflicted. Now, if I toed the line and conformed to the oppressive norms of traditional Indian culture, it wasn't because I was afraid of my dad; it was because I didn't want to cause turbulence in my parents' relationship. This became a double emotional burden that I wasn't even aware of at the time. In those days, in my culture, a woman didn't leave her parents' home until she got married, so my simply getting a job and moving out was not an option available to me. My father's and my rocky relationship continued until he passed. Our issues weren't resolved until I encountered him on the other side during my NDE.

Shattering the Glass Ceiling

When I died, I realized that there's no gender in the other realm. There's no gender because we have no biology. We're just pure spiritual beings. We're magnificent beyond belief. We're strong, we're powerful. These qualities are all part of who we are, all part of loving ourselves, all part of the universal consciousness. We want to embrace them in our physical life. Our empathy and sensitivity as well as our assertiveness, our masculinity as well as our femininity—it's all equally important in forming the whole that is each of us: Think of the concept, for example, of yin and yang. There's no judgment in that realm about which of these qualities is more positive or negative. In fact, there's absolutely no judgment in that realm. Period!

This awareness felt so real! It felt so right! Something hadn't felt right when I was growing up, but during my NDE, I had total clarity about these things, and it made so much sense.

I realized that the roles we play, the roles we stick to—the gender roles that have been taught to us—are simply cultural roles. The roles that we carry emotionally—the guilt that women carry if we go to work outside the home; the self-sacrifice (as opposed to self-love) that we're taught to embrace; the suppression of the ego, which women are encouraged to strive for more than men—all these are cultural conditionings. But seeing the other realm showed me how possible—and fantastic—it is to be free of cultural and gender restrictions.

My husband, Danny, had always been better at housework than I was, but before I died, instead of seeing it as a wonderful skill Danny had, I saw it as a deficiency in myself. It was a source of embarrassment to me, one I always tried to cover up when friends and family visited. However, after my experience in the other realm, I proudly boast about how fabulous Danny is at running our home, while he enjoys poking fun at my domestic incompetence (with humor, of course).

Here on Earth, both genders are equally important. As with yin and yang, one without the other creates an imbalance. As one who is an empath, and therefore more emotional than other people, I encourage you to embrace all your superpowers as your strengths. Whether you're a man or woman, transgender, gay, or straight—embrace them all. We label our sensitivities as feminine qualities, and they are, but in a "yin" sort of way. We don't have to give these qualities a gender; they're equally as important as those "yang" qualities so valued in our current paradigm, qualities such as being assertive, headstrong, stubborn, aggressive, and tough.

There are a lot of empathic men who embrace these more sensitive qualities, but they're afraid to show it because they're afraid of being labeled as weak. On the other hand, there are women who believe they need to become more like men to succeed in this world. I want you to know that's not true. Today, we need these feminine qualities more than ever.

We need more women in role-model roles. We need more strong women who are embracing feminine qualities as role models for the rest of us. I encourage you to embrace your ego because you need your ego to take on leadership roles. Your ego isn't your enemy. The enemy is in suppressing your spiritual awareness, your inner mystic, and your connection to the web of consciousness. As an empath, with your spiritual awareness and incredible empathy, you need to embrace your ego to know that your message is important and needs to be shared, on whatever scale you choose.

One of the things I've learned is to always work toward being unapologetically authentic—regardless of my gender. I invite you to do the same. Embrace who you are. Embrace your strengths and gifts. On the other hand, if you're lousy at something—such as math or spelling—don't be afraid to admit it. I'm hoping that you'll find, as I have, that the more you can accept yourself without judgment, the less you'll fear judgment from others. And in doing so, you can bring your strengths forward.

Meditation for Embracing Your Gender

You have so much to contribute. These words will help you to welcome all that you are—the yin and yang of you.

> *"As I relax into my body*
> *I realize there's a reason I am who I am.*
> *I am perfect in my gender.*
> *Everything about me is needed and valued in this physical life.*
> *I allow myself to express myself fully and authentically.*
> *I embrace my strengths unapologetically.*
> *I embrace and nurture my body unashamedly."*

Chapter 11

LIVING FEARLESSLY

MANTRA:
"I live my life fearlessly!"

When I died, my dad told me to go forth and live my life fearlessly, and I have. As I learned during my NDE, that's all we're here to do—be ourselves, love who we are, and live our life from that place. Living fearlessly is the expression of our true selves. This means accepting our thoughts, both negative and positive. In our five-sensory paradigm, we all suppress certain thoughts that don't align with the accepted way of thinking. After working with so many empaths, I've found that we also suppress our thoughts because of our ability to read others. We believe they can read us as easily as we can read them. So we bury our more telling thoughts, put a protective shell around ourselves, and hide.

Then there's the whole tyranny of negative thinking—the idea that if we think anything negative, even for a fleeting moment, we'll manifest it. This fear can be especially pervasive for empaths because we're so susceptible to the power of suggestion. When I was in the throes of dealing with the challenge of cancer, everyone was talking about the

Law of Attraction. It was huge. I can't tell you the number of people who said things like, "You attracted the cancer." "Your thoughts attracted the cancer." "Negative thoughts attract a negative reality." I couldn't understand it. How could that be? I'd always been a very positive person. I was always the one who was joyful, the one who everyone came to if they needed some positive reinforcement. I had friends who were sometimes sullen or moody, or even bitchy—but that was never me. I was always the one who cheered everyone up. I wanted everyone to like me, remember?

When we try and suppress our thoughts and emotions, the message we send to ourselves is *I'm not good enough, so I need to annihilate this part of myself*. We suppress a part of who we truly are, and this is unhealthy. To monitor each and every thought—squashing or allowing them one by one—requires judging our thoughts, and when we do that, we're judging ourselves. It's a more contrived, rather than authentic, way of being.

This is what we have to watch out for when following these beliefs about the Law of Attraction without fully understanding them. I don't believe we attract people, events, and circumstances to us by our *thoughts*. Instead, I believe we attract what comes our way by *who we are* at any given time.

I didn't truly understand the Law of Attraction until I died and learned that loving yourself for exactly who you are is the key. When you love and value yourself, you no longer have to watch your thoughts.

Be Who You Are!

I know from my own experience that when you allow yourself to be who you are, you accept even your negative thoughts without fear. They come through you, and they pass. These negative thoughts, just like the positive ones, are simply part of who you are, and when we allow ourselves to be who we are, we attract what's truly ours. We don't have to worry about our thoughts or how to hold on to positive outcomes, opportunities, relationships, and experiences when we attract them, or fear our negative thoughts when we're going through a rough time. They're just thoughts, and all of them contribute to making you who you are.

Now I don't even label my thoughts as positive or negative—they're just me. And you'll get to this same place. Think about young children. They blurt out all kinds of negative thoughts, and then they're on to the next thing, the next game. They don't attract cataclysmic outcomes. You don't judge them. They don't judge themselves. They know they're still loved. They're learning. And so are we. So give yourself some slack. Just love yourself. Be yourself.

The way to truly be yourself is to ask yourself, *If I were creating myself anew, who would I be? Who would I be if no one were watching?* As you ask yourself these questions, remember that you're no longer navigating your life with your eyes closed, as we discussed in Chapter 1. You're no longer in a five-sensory world. You're looking at the world through fresh eyes. So how do you see yourself now, without all your beliefs about how things should be? How do you experience yourself? If you're not sure, you might pose the question to your inner mystic: *Do I want to see myself as someone who's light, who's free, who's successful, who's creative?* Then see what image comes up for you.

The reason we attract things we don't want in our lives is not because of negative thoughts but because we're creating our reality through our baggage and beliefs from the past. Once we let go of all that, by listening to our inner mystic and loving who we are, we begin to view the world through this place of clarity. We create the life we want, and allow the world to mirror it back to us.

How we view the world is dependent on the lens through which we view it, and when we shift our beliefs, which means changing the lens, our view changes. In other words, if we view the world through a more benevolent lens, that's what we'll see more of. If we view the world with anger, that's what's reflected back to us. For example, when you buy a new car, you suddenly notice a bombardment of the same car, even though you hadn't seen any, or very few, of them around before you drove off the lot. Or, say you buy an unusual color of car, just to be different, and then you suddenly notice how many others are driving a car of a similar color. My first car was bright red. I didn't think there were that many red cars on the road, but after getting my red car, wow!

On a more esoteric level, there's scientific evidence about how we affect our environment. Think about Dr. Masaru Emoto's book *The Hidden Messages in Water,* in which he outlines his experiments with water. He found that thoughts and feelings, a state of being, and music, affect physical reality—in this case, the shape of crystals in frozen water.[1] And in 1998, researchers at the Weizmann Institute of Science conducted a highly controlled experiment demonstrating how a beam of electrons is affected by the act of being observed. The experiment revealed that the greater the amount of time "watching," the greater the observer's influence on what actually takes place.[2]

It was made very clear to me in that NDE state that it's not *just* my thoughts that are responsible for creating my reality, it's also honoring and loving *who I am.* The only thing I need to do is to be myself. Fearlessly. Being fearlessly yourself means loving yourself enough to allow yourself to live without your baggage and beliefs, without seeing the world the way others do, or would have you see it. It means not needing approval from them to feel worthy, not needing an illness as an excuse to take care of yourself, not having to justify being yourself. It means knowing you're worthy and deserving without having to prove yourself.

In a nutshell, it's *fear* that prevented me from being who I am (fear of being disliked, fear of disapproval, fear of not being worthy or good enough), and it's *love* that helps me be myself. The more I love myself, the more I realize I'm worthy and deserving of expressing myself without apology. That's how it works. The more you allow yourself to be who you are, the more you send yourself the message *I love myself, and there's nothing wrong with me.*

So allow yourself to be authentic, to be who you truly are. When you do, you're also telling yourself there's nothing wrong with your thoughts. Even when you have the occasional negative or fear-based thought, you can allow it. You can take the attitude of *Hey, it's a part of me. Let's see what it says. And then it'll leave when it's done.* This feels so much better than *Oh my God. I have to suppress this negative thought because it's going to attract a negative reality*—fearing the thought, and then fearing the fear because it might generate more thoughts . . . All the while you're judging yourself for having these thoughts in the first place.

How can you escape your inner fears so that you can stop putting up obstacles to being who you truly are? In other words, how can you go from fear of being yourself to loving yourself?

Understand where fear comes from. Fears usually come from the outside. Even though you may feel these are inner fears because they're fears in your mind, that's not how it works. Because when you go deep inside, there's only love. *Only love.* Our current global reality seems to be at an imbalance, where it's being run more by fear than by love, and a lot of you reading this are empaths, so you're feeling it more deeply. Because of this, you may very well believe that these are your inner fears. But they're not—they're coming from our current external paradigm.

Try minimizing input from the outside world. We discussed unplugging in Chapter 3. You can also take time out from people who are triggering your fears.

Consult your inner mystic. Whenever you feel fear, it's a call to go inward. Although your purpose is to be here in this physical world, in this physical body, and not to escape it, our paradigm can sometimes become too noisy and fearful. This can bring us out of balance. Spending time connecting with our inner world can correct that. It's about getting back in touch with our soul's calling and intention, and the love that drew you forth into this world in the first place.

Love and Cherish Who You Are!

I've talked about how to love yourself, and how you can love yourself more, and now I want to explain how to call on your inner guidance to help you. You can start by asking questions such as *How can I love myself more? How can I allow myself to be more authentic? Where can I release fear?* So, again, living an authentic life is not about watching your thoughts and being fearful of your thoughts. It's about *Okay, how can I love myself more?*

If you're going through an illness, a depression, or a negative period in your life, you never want to tell yourself, *You attracted this* or *Your negative thoughts attracted your reality* or *Don't be so negative.* That's the last thing you want to say. What you do want to say if you're going through pain, hurt, confusion, fear, or an illness is, *Hey, this is an invitation for me to love myself more, to allow more good things in my life.* Ask yourself, *How can I do that? How can I find more joy in myself, in my life? What are the things that make me happy?*

This focus will help you be more authentic, which is important because, as I've just said, we attract who we really are. So when you're joyful you allow more joy to come into your life. And the way to be more joyful is to love yourself more, so that you're not so judgmental about your thoughts. You can use this same technique when supporting others who are going through a difficult time.

One way of being more loving toward yourself is to talk to yourself in a whole new way. Instead of judging yourself, or being angry with yourself for going through a health challenge or difficult period, I would encourage you to treat yourself as your own best friend. If your best friend were going through what you're going through, what would you say to him or her? Perhaps something along the lines of, "Don't be afraid. I'm here for you" or "This will pass and you'll be stronger for it" or "I'll love you through this." I encourage you to tune in to your inner guidance, ask yourself these questions, and listen for the answers. If they resonate with you, then take action.

You always want to bring yourself to a space where you're feeling more loved. Always, always. You want to show yourself that you need to learn to accept yourself more and love yourself more. That's how you shift into a higher frequency. Here's the idea behind shifting into a higher frequency, or vibration. We know that everything is made of energy. According to the Law of Vibration, that energy is always in a state of vibration. That includes every part of you. The higher the vibration, the lighter, more intuitive, and more aware you feel. You don't get to a higher frequency by fearing your thoughts, but by accepting them. You also want to help others who are struggling accept and love themselves more. Doing so raises both your frequencies. Just remember, love is the answer to every single problem in the world. Love is the solution to everything.

Empaths love to bring joy and happiness and light to those around us, and this is why we go around rescuing people and helping people. We love to uplift others. To do so, we need to love ourselves. This is why my slogan is "Love yourself like your life depends on it, because it does!" For me, learning to love myself was a very expensive lesson that almost took my life.

Empaths really need to be encouraged to feel that it's not selfish to love ourselves or fulfill our needs. In fact, it's selfish *not* to, because we only end up contributing to the problem. Yet when you take care of yourself first, you may encounter people who will see that as selfish. In my earlier days of sharing my story about my NDE and healing from cancer, I sometimes found people saying (particularly on social media) something to the effect of, "At least you have the luxury of taking care of your own needs. There are people who are suffering, people who are so poor/sick/dying! How does it help them if you believe that the most important thing you can do is to love yourself?"

But that thinking is backward. Sometimes I still feel a twinge of guilt when people say this to me. Yet it's common in my line of work. People expect utter sacrifice from those with a spiritual message. It can be hard to change the mindset of those who believe that true service means sacrifice of self. People expect the same type of selflessness from healers, too, and also from teachers, parents, leaders, and in the culture in which I grew up, definitely from women. When I come up against someone with these beliefs, someone who calls me out for seeing to my own needs, I remind myself that if I don't love myself, or take care of myself, and if I don't listen to my own inner guidance and intuition, then I will reap the consequences, which could be getting sick. And if I'm sick, or suffering, or even dying as a consequence of not taking care of myself, what good am I to others? Instead of being part of the solution, I become part of the problem.

Allowing Instead of Attracting

Living fearlessly means being *who you are* fearlessly, and opening yourself up to possibilities you never imagined without self-imposed limits to contain you, bring order, and help keep a lid on fear. Sometimes people ask me about my views on setting goals. For most situations, I'm not a big fan of them. I believe that the goals we come up with can restrict us. We're capable of achieving far more than we realize, and we can't grasp what we can do because we're unaware of the whole of who we are. Our views are limited to what we can see, which is our physical bodies.

The key is understanding who you are—recognizing that your physical self is not *all* that you are. Look down at your body and see it for what it is. What I want you to realize, really get, is that this body is just the tip of an iceberg. The 20 percent. The remaining 80 percent of you is in the other realm. You can't see it with your physical eyes, but it exists. Our energies expand so far that they connect with the energies of everyone around us. However, we interact in this world and with others as though all of us are purely the tips of the iceberg—that is, purely a physical body in this time and space, and nothing more.

When I speak about six-sensory beings or being aware of your six-sensory self, it means being aware of that 80 percent that you can't see. The other 80 percent of us is capable of so much more than we can imagine. That's what it felt like when I died. I saw and felt it all. There was a *lot* more of me that was *not* physical than there was of me that *was*. I wasn't just the visible tip of the iceberg; I was, in fact, the whole iceberg. I was enormous and magnificent beyond description!

When we realize that our physical self is only a teeny part of the whole of who we are, we become aware that everyone we've ever met in this world is only a sliver of who *they* really are. At that point, we understand the minuteness of everything we've fought about, worried over, and argued about. We also realize we've been making big issues out of tiny problems because we fail to see that the visible self is just a tiny part of something much, much bigger, something far beyond what our five senses can see or hear.

Recently, I received a letter from someone who asked, "What if you have a huge, huge desire in life? Where does this desire come from, and what should you do about it? Is it correct to try and focus on it with your thoughts and feelings, i.e., apply the Law of Attraction? Am I limiting myself if I do that?" My response is that when you create your vision or your desire for your future from your current position, your vision is limited to what you can see or what you know right now.

Let me give you an example from my own life. When I was going through my illness, my greatest desire was to get well, and I started creating vision boards. This was in 2005, before digital vision boards caught on. I bought a corkboard, cut pictures of healthy people out of magazines, and created a collage. Working on my vision board was great for a while, but when I didn't see the vibrant health or even improvement manifesting in my body, I became more fearful. The thing about vision boards is that if you don't see your desire manifesting in the way you want it to, you start to feel fear and doubt. And when you start to feel fear, you lose that original place of love and inspiration that you started with.

If I'm going through a difficult time, it means that my present moment is not going the way I'd hoped. You don't want to create from that place. If you're feeling angry, scared, or frustrated in the present moment, you kick into survival mode, and you're closed off to inspiration. Our creative juices stop flowing when we're in survival mode, so we can't envision a good outcome. Instead, try focusing on figuring out what could make this moment better, even if it's a baby step. No matter the condition of your life, figure out what could improve, whether it means spending some time with loved ones, time alone, time listening to music, connecting with your higher self, asking what the situation or moment is trying to tell or show you, or even just asking yourself, *Who would I be if no one were watching?* That's what I do.

A woman wrote to me saying that she used to use vision boards and followed all the protocols set out by Law of Attraction theorists, but she never got the desired results. And then, after watching one of my videos, she realized she was coming at it from a place of fear, scarcity, and survival, so this was the lens through which she was creating. She then shifted her focus to just trying to feel better in that moment, and as she continued to do that for each moment moving forward, she felt she was in a much better place to create a more expansive future. So much so that she soon felt she didn't even need tools like vision boards, because she was only leaning on them during her fear-based phase.

Looking back at my life now, I can see that the desired reality I pinned to my vision board was limited compared to the future my dharma (true divine purpose) had in store for me. That future was much, much bigger than what I could ever have imagined at that time—particularly because I was coming at it from a place of fear and survival.

Just like the lower 80 percent of the iceberg, we can't imagine what we can't yet see. So if we set goals, or even create vision boards, we may be frustrating and limiting ourselves with that restricted vision of what's in store for us, because we can't see all of who we truly are.

There may be a future waiting for you that's greater than you can imagine, and most of us are incapable of imagining something greater than what we currently know. So your only job is to love your current self and find joy in this current moment. If you're not feeling joy, do what lifts your spirits so that you feel at your most elevated self. For example, if I'm feeling stressed about a situation that looks like it's turning bad, I may remove myself physically and focus on something completely different—go for a walk on the beach, cook a meal, take a shower, or any number of things that I really enjoy doing. When I'm doing any of these things, I find myself in a space of clarity, and life always feels much better. Consequently, I'm in a better place to deal with the situation. As long as you do the best you can with the present moment, you'll be allowing the best possible future to unfold.

The images I pinned to my vision board didn't come close to the life I'm living today. I could never have imagined this life. I didn't even know such a life existed! So don't limit yourself. Don't limit yourself with goals, the exact details of how your future will look, or the exact outcome of a project you're working on. Leave it open-ended. Your only job is to express fully in this moment. To be fearless in this moment. To find your joy and your expanded self in this moment.

Now, on to how to do that . . .

Loving the Self Means Loving the Whole

When I tell people to love themselves, I usually need to tell them about the 80 percent, because for the most part, they're only aware of and love the tip of their iceberg, the self they can see. "Hey, I get massages," people will sometimes tell me if they haven't heard my full message. "I go get regular cuts/color/highlights. I get facials. I work out. I take care of myself.

How come my life is still such a struggle and how come I still don't feel I love myself?" I then explain to them what's going on: "The reason you don't feel you love yourself is because you're neglecting 80 percent of yourself. You're only loving the other 20 percent."

The first step toward fully loving yourself is to become aware that there *is* another 80 percent and that you're actually a six-sensory being. Then, tune in to that 80 percent, because that part knows your purpose. That's the part of you that you need to love, accept, know, and trust. And when you do, the nonphysical and physical parts of you integrate.

Right now, it might feel as though the nonphysical and physical are two separate things. You may feel you're just an iceberg floating in the ocean, because you can't see what's underneath. That's why you feel lost, lonely, and isolated; because that tip is all you can see. But if you could see the whole thing, the magnificence that's below the surface and con-nected to everything else—the rest of the world, the other icebergs, the water, the earth, the elements—and become aware that you're so much greater than you were previously aware, you could get in touch with that part of yourself. For you, the way to get in touch might be to go on a retreat, listen to spiritual podcasts, play a musical instrument, cook a delicious meal, paint a picture—whatever puts you in touch with that greater part of you.

Throughout the day, wherever I am, I talk to the rest of my iceberg. I get in touch with it when I'm lying in bed at night before I fall asleep. Once you love, accept, know, and trust that part that is your soul—once you talk to it, nourish it by acknowledging that *Yes, there's so much more to me. Yes, that part of me is trying to guide me all the time. Yes, it knows my calling and why I'm here. It knows what's in store for me in my future. It's trying to call me to my future self*—it talks to you, and you stop feeling lost. That's truly what happens. That's what happened with me; it's what the NDE did for me: It made me aware of the whole iceberg. And that's what I invite you to do. Tap in. It's that simple.

If you have children and you want them to remember the magnitude of who they truly are, the best thing you can do is to make them aware that their physical body is just the tip of the iceberg, and that there's so much more to them than what they can physically see—*so* much more. Teach them to get in tune with their whole self, including the 80 percent they can't see, by encouraging them to trust their feelings and their intuition. Let them know that they can engage with this 80 percent by asking questions and listening for the answers. Ask them how they *feel* in different situations, to move them from their head space into their heart space.

The heart is more in tune with our 80 percent. For example, if your kids are watching a movie or a TV show, or playing a game, it's important for them to acknowledge not just how it's stimulating their mind, but how they're feeling. Ask them what they're feeling. Are they feeling anxious when they watch certain shows, or play certain games? Fearful? Joyful? Ask how they feel when they study certain subjects at school—not just what grades they're getting in that subject, but how it makes them feel. How do they feel about being in the school playground at recess, or going to birthday parties or other social situations? Anxious? Fearful? Or joyful with a feeling of anticipation? Understanding what your child is feeling is a good doorway to getting in touch with their 80 percent, and helping them to do the same.

If a child is getting bullied at school, it's just the tip of the iceberg that's being bullied, and they need to get in tune with their whole self. They also need to realize that the bully is only coming from the tip of *their* iceberg. The bully is coming from a place of weakness. There's so much more to that person but they don't realize it. They don't see their own greatness. So they need to diminish others in order to feel great. That's basically what a bully does.

When you're in touch with the entire iceberg, you experience the integration and wholeness. I know I've said that loving and accepting yourself are crucial, but at this point I want to zoom out to look at the bigger picture, when you reach the point of *Oh my God, I get it. I don't have to focus on loving myself. Because there is no self. There's no physical self.*

I want to focus on loving the whole. It's a natural progression. You understand that you're part of this eternal self, part of the greater entity, which is the whole iceberg that's connected to the entire Universe. It has all the answers to everything. For me, when I sit in quiet meditation, when I go out in nature, when I'm having my shower, that's when I connect to this greater self, and it's where I get my answers.

When you start listening to that higher part of you, that's when your life unfolds in the way it's meant to. That's when you really start to listen to who you are, and do what you're here to do. It's not about trying to be what everyone else wants you to be, to fit into the dominant paradigm. I really had to learn to put that into practice.

Today, I wouldn't trade anything about the way my life has panned out; meeting Wayne Dyer in 2011 and everything that's happened since then—traveling all over the world and meeting so many people; being given an opportunity to share my story with such welcoming audiences and helping them to see their physical illnesses differently and alleviate some of their fears; and, most important, connecting with amazing people like you, as well as other speakers and teachers doing similar work. Rebuilding my tribe. None of it would have happened if I didn't believe in what I believe in, if I didn't follow my heart the way I did, and still do. It just wouldn't have happened.

Think about it: What lies in store for you if you follow your heart and allow yourself to be all that you can be, fearlessly?

Meditation for Being Yourself, Unapologetically

As you begin living your life fearlessly, you might want to try this meditation daily for a while. It opens up the space for expanding into who you are with a deep feeling of self-love and peace, the best place to be when putting yourself out in the world, standing up for what you believe in, and saying to the Universe, "Bring it on! Show me what's next."

> *"As I move through each day*
> *I allow myself to be who I am without judgment.*
> *I allow my thoughts to flow without condemnation.*
> *I embrace who I am in each given moment.*
> *If I feel fear, I lovingly hold and assure myself without suppressing*
> *the thoughts*
> *Until the fear has dissipated.*
> *I allow myself the space to be me."*

Speak your truth. Open the door for a whole new way of being.
Set in motion the shift our planet needs to heal and survive.

ACKNOWLEDGMENTS

For me, this is one of the most important parts of this book. It's where I get to express my gratitude to everyone who, in some way or other, has been an integral part of my journey and who was involved—either directly or indirectly—in bringing this book into being.

First and foremost, I'd like to thank my agent extraordinaire, Stephanie Tade. She really is the best agent anyone can have. Not only did she rescue me from a precarious visa situation, she also landed me a wonderful book deal with Simon & Schuster and brought me the most magical editor I could ever ask for! Thank you, Stephanie. You are the best!

Speaking of editors, this book would not exist without the magical way in which Kelly Malone helped me bring it together! She is an empath and related to everything I wanted it to be. She has a way of really tapping into my mind that got my creativity flowing onto the pages! Kelly, I just cannot thank you enough, and I'm so grateful the stars aligned to bring you into my life as my editor for this very important book. The experience of bringing these pages into fruition was made so easy with you in my corner championing me!

I would also like to thank the beautiful Zhena Muzyka for welcoming my book to its home at Simon & Schuster. Zhena, you are such a generous and gifted connector of people, and a true unicorn if I ever met one! Thank you for being in my life and becoming a friend.

Also, to Debra Olivier, thank you so much for all your help in getting me started on this manuscript! I learned so much from you and am so grateful for the foundation of this book you helped me build, which allowed it to grow and flourish into what it has become.

To Daniella Wexler and Loan Le, my wonderful editors at Simon & Schuster—thank you so much for your dedication, patience, and hard work to help me bring this book into being, and for recognizing how important this work is to me. Thank you for also seeing it through to the finish line!

To my fabulous team who work with me behind the scenes, keeping all the cogs and gears running, going above and beyond the call of duty, particularly Roz and Milena.

And finally, last but not least, thanks to my darling husband and boo, Danny. It has been a joy to share this world, this time-space reality, and this existence with you. I'm so blessed to have you in my life and love you to eternity and back. You are the reason behind everything I do, the wind beneath my wings.

I'd also like to thank every single empath on this planet, especially the ones who have written to me or said to me over the years that they see themselves in me and my experiences. Thank you for being the inspiration behind this book. I'd also like to express my gratitude to every one of *you* who are holding this book in your hands, as well as those of you who have written to me. I am so grateful to all of you for all your support, your letters, and your outpouring of love. Without you, I wouldn't be doing what I am doing today.

NOTES

Introduction

1 Christiane Northrup, MD, "8 Ways to Turn Your Empathy into a Super Power," accessed March 21, 2018, https://www.drnorthrup.com/8-ways-to-turn-your-empathy-into-a-super-power/.

Chapter 1: Are You an Empath?

1 Elaine N. Aron, PhD, The *Highly Sensitive Person: How to Thrive When the World Overwhelms You* (Toronto: Citadel Press, 2013), Kindle edition, loc. 561.

2 Judith Orloff, MD, *The Empath's Survival Guide: Life Strategies for Sensitive People* (Boulder, CO: Sounds True, 2017), Kindle edition, loc. 59.

Chapter 3: How to Live Life More Optimally as an Empath

1 Dr. Joe Dispenza, *You Are the Placebo: Making Your Mind Matter* (Carlsbad, CA: Hay House, 2014), Kindle edition, loc. 1166. 47.

2 Judith Orloff, MD, *The Empath's Survival Guide*, loc. 104.

3 Ibid., loc 108.

4 Matt Kahn, *Everything Here Is to Help You: A Loving Guide to Your Soul's Evolution* (Carlsbad: Hay House, 2018), Kindle edition, loc. 77.

5 William Butler Yeats, *The Winding Stair and Other Poems: A Facsimile Edition* (New York: Scribner, 2011), 81.

Chapter 4: Turning Up the Dial on Your Ego

1   Anita Moorjani, *What If This Is Heaven? How Our Cultural Myths Prevent Us from Experiencing Heaven on Earth* (Carlsbad, CA: Hay House, 2016), Kindle edition, 174.

2   Gabor Maté, MD, *When the Body Says No: Exploring the Stress-Disease Connection* (Hoboken, NJ: Wiley, 2011) Kindle edition, loc. 307.

3   Harriet Brown, "The Boom and Bust Ego: The Less You Think about Your Own Self-Esteem, the Healthier You'll Be," *Psychology Today*, January 1, 2012, https://www.psychologytoday.com/us/articles/201201/the-boom-and-bust-ego.

4   Brian Johnson, "Three Perspectives on Addiction," *Journal of the American Psychiatric Organization*, June 1, 1999, https://journals.sagepub.com/doi/pdf/10.1177/00030651990470031301.

5   Edith Eva Eger, PhD, *The Choice: Embrace the Possible* (New York: Scribner, 2017), Kindle edition, 116.

Chapter 6: When the Body Rebels

1   Judith Orloff, MD, *The Empath's Survival Guide*, loc. 2509.

2   Bruce H. Lipton, PhD, "Mind, Growth, and Matter," June 7, 2012, https://www.brucelipton.com/resource/interview/mind-growth-and-matter.

3   Esther Hicks, Abraham Hicks (workshop, October 2, 2004, Boston, Massachusetts), https://www.abraham-hickslawofattraction.com/2004102-boston-ma-mp3-complete-workshop-recording.html.

4   Albert Einstein, *Einstein on Cosmic Religion and Other Opinions and Aphorisms* (Mineola, NY: Dover Publications, 2012), Kindle edition, loc. 356.

5   Kelly Noonan Gores, *Heal: Discover Your Unlimited Potential and Awaken the Powerful Healer Within* (New York: Atria Books, 2019), 4.

6   Bruce H. Lipton, PhD, *The Biology of Belief* (Carlsbad, CA: Hay House, 2015), 10th Anniversary Edition, 118, Kindle edition, loc. 2119.

7   Dr. Joe Dispenza, *You Are the Placebo*, 131.

Chapter 8: Opening to Abundance without Guilt

1   "Better Quality of Work Life Is Worth a $7,600 Pay Cut to Millennials," April 7, 2016, Fidelity, https://www.fidelity.com/about-fidelity/individual-investing/better-quality-of-work-life-is-worth-pay-cut-for-millennials.

2   Tiziana Barghini, "Inequality," *Global Finance*, January 1, 2019, https://www.gfmag.com/magazine/january-2019/inequality.

3   Wayne Dyer, *The Power of Intention: Learning to Co-create Your World Your Way* (Carlsbad, CA: Hay House, 2006), Kindle edition, loc. 2932.

Chapter 9: Saying "Yes" to Saying "No"

1 Benjamin P. Chapman et al., "Emotion Suppression and Mortality Risk Over a 12-Year Follow-up," *Journal of Psychosomatic Research*, 75, no. 4 (October 2013): 381–385, https://www.ncbi.nlm.nih.gov/pmc/articles/PMC3939772/.

Chapter 10: Breaking Through Gender Norms

1 Emma Newburger, "Closing the Gap: A New Study Shows that Women Earn Half of What Men Earn," *CNBC Make It*, November 28, 2018, https://www.cnbc.com/2018/11/28/study-for-every-dollar-a-man-earns-a-woman-earns-49-cents.html.

2 "Global Gender Gap Report 2018," World Economic Forum, https://reports.weforum.org/global-gender-gap-report-2018/key-findings/.

Chapter 11: Living Fearlessly

1 Masaru Emoto, *The Hidden Messages in Water* (New York: Atria Books, 2011), Kindle edition, loc. 127–149.

2 Weizmann Institute of Science, "Quantum Theory Demonstrated: Observation Affects Reality," *ScienceDaily*, February 27, 1998, https://www.sciencedaily.com/releases/1998/02/980227055013.htm.

ABOUT THE AUTHOR

Anita Moorjani, *New York Times* best-selling author of *Dying to Be Me* and more recently *What If This Is Heaven?*, is a woman with a remarkable story! After a four-year battle with cancer, Anita fell into a coma and was given hours to live. As her doctors gathered to revive her, she journeyed into a near death experience (NDE), during which she was given the choice to return to her physical form or to continue into this new realm. She chose the former, and when she regained consciousness, her cancer began to heal. To the amazement of her doctors, she was free of countless tumors and cancer indicators within weeks.

Her book *Dying to Be Me* has sold more than a million copies worldwide, in more than forty-five languages. It has been named a "contemporary classic" and a "foreign language phenomenon" by her publisher Hay House Inc. It has now also been optioned by Hollywood producers to be made into a full-length feature film.

Anita was a protégé of the late, great Dr. Wayne Dyer, who brought her onto the world's stage in 2011. She is an amazing speaker and has gone on to capture the hearts and attention of millions across the globe. She has also been a featured guest on *The Dr. Oz Show*, Fox News, the *Today* show, CNN's *Anderson Cooper 360°*, the National Geographic Channel's special feature *Life After Life*, *The Pearl Report* in Hong Kong, *Headstart with Karen Davila* in the Philippines, and many others. The

UK's prestigious publication *Watkins MIND BODY SPIRIT Magazine* has listed Anita among the top one hundred of "The World's Most Spiritually Influential Living People" for the eighth consecutive year.

Anita has dedicated her life to empowering the minds and hearts of people with her story of courage and transformation. She travels the world speaking her truth with grace and humor to sold-out audiences who want to learn of her journey and experiences of embracing change, the power of healing, and the quest to live a full and unlimited life.

Today, Anita lives in the United States with her husband, Danny, and continues to share her incredible story and lessons internationally. Prior to her cancer diagnosis, Anita lived and worked in Hong Kong with her husband. She was born in Singapore of Indian parents and grew up speaking English, Cantonese, and an Indian dialect simultaneously.

Visit Anita's website to learn about her online community, watch her weekly Facebook Live videos, and get tips about how to embrace your gifts and thrive as an empath. www.anitamoorjani.com